SELLING YOUR CHURCH IN THE '90S

A Public Relations Guide for Clergy and Laity

Boyce A. Bowdon

Koinonia Press
Oklahoma City, OK

Cover designed by Jim Rice
Illustrated by Curtis Boles

Unless otherwise noted, all scripture quotations are from the New Revised Standard Version of the Holy Bible, Copyright © 1989 by the Division of Christian Education of the National Council of Churches of Christ in the USA and used by permission.

ISBN 0-9632495-0-9

SELLING YOUR CHURCH IN THE '90S: A PUBLIC RELATIONS GUIDE FOR CLERGY AND LAITY. Copyright © 1992 by Boyce A. Bowdon. All rights reserved. Printed in the United States of America by Koinonia Press in cooperation with the Office of Conference Services and Communication Education of United Methodist Communications. No part of this book may be reproduced in any manner whatsoever without written permission except in the case of brief quotations embodied in critical articles or reviews. For information, address Koinonia Press, P. O. Box 57244, Oklahoma City, OK 75157.

To my wife, Arlene, my best friend ever

CONTENTS

Acknowledgments   7

Introduction   8

CHAPTER 1:
Discovering a Sense of Mission   11

CHAPTER 2:
Finding a New Identity   14

CHAPTER 3:
Empowering Lay Ministry   19

CHAPTER 4:
Building Positive Response with PR   24

CHAPTER 5:
Prospecting for Members   36

CHAPTER 6:
Advertising Effectively   42

CHAPTER 7:
Enhancing Your Church's Image   51

CHAPTER 8:
Ministering Through Video and Audio Media   57

CHAPTER 9:
Upgrading Church Publications   67

CHAPTER 10:
Working with the Media   81

CHAPTER 11:
Slowing the Rumor Mill   93

CHAPTER 12:
  Managing Conflict   98

CHAPTER 13:
  Initiating Change   103

CHAPTER 14:
  Reflections: It Will Pay Off in the Long Run   106

Endnotes   110

Suggested Reading   112

ACKNOWLEDGMENTS

Clergy and laypersons of seven denominations have made valuable contributions to the development of this book.

I am especially grateful to the following:

- Participants in church communications and public relations workshops that I have conducted during the past decade. They challenged me to focus on questions that clergy and laypersons face, and they helped me find solutions.
- Persons across the country who have told me how they are selling their churches and who have permitted me to share their case studies. Their insights and experiences have added depth and made this book more practical.
- My brother, Foster Bowdon, a certified public accountant in Jonesboro, Arkansas, who encouraged me to write this book. When I was a teenager, Foster sold me on the church. While helping him with lay speaking assignments, I received my call to the ministry. I have never known a man with a more Christlike spirit.

INTRODUCTION

TRINITY CHURCH MUST BE SOLD.

That headline grabbed my attention one morning in 1973 as I glanced at a newsletter from Trinity United Methodist Church in Atlanta.

The article reported that more than three hundred church members had voted to abandon Trinity. It announced that a meeting would be held to explore how the church could be sold.

Less than a month had passed since I had been in Atlanta, where I had visited Ken Jones, the pastor of Trinity, looking for insights that might help me as pastor of St. Andrew's United Methodist Church in Oklahoma City.

Our two churches had much in common. Both had thrived during the 1950s, but were struggling to survive in the 1970s due to changes that had occurred in their respective neighborhoods.

Under Ken's leadership, Trinity was reviving. People were excited. They had a sense of mission. New members were joining. The building, which was located in the heart of downtown Atlanta, was being renovated and becoming a hub of activity.

I returned home inspired, and my people were encouraged when I shared with them what was happening at Trinity. We believed that what was happening there could happen at St. Andrew's.

You can imagine how disappointed I was when I read that Trinity was for sale. What had gone wrong? I decided to call Ken and find out.

When he answered the phone, and I told him why I had called, he began to chuckle.

"Every word in the article is true," he said. "Three hundred members voted to abandon the church—they stopped attending. And Trinity must be sold. The building is not for sale, but the church is. Unless it is sold—unless people assume ownership of it—it won't be long until we have to close our doors. We will meet Sunday afternoon to talk about ways we can do a better selling job."

I called Ken back the next week to find out what had happened at the meeting. Again, he was chuckling.

"People came who hadn't been to the church in years," he said. "They wanted to know why we were selling the dear old church where they had grown up, been baptized, married, and had other life-shaping experiences."

Introduction

Ken said that after he had clarified what he meant by announcing that the church was for sale that even those who didn't think his attention-getting gimmick was amusing saw the point he was making.

THE CHURCH MUST BE SOLD

After twenty centuries—despite vicious attacks by critics and tyrants and despite colossal weaknesses of members and leaders—the church is still alive. There is only one way to explain its survival and impact: God's grace—not human achievement—keeps it viable.

The church is a gift of God; but it is not God. Therefore, selling the church is not an end in itself. Instead, it is a means toward helping people experience God's love; heightening their love for God, for themselves, and for one another; and bolstering their commitment as disciples of Jesus Christ.

Fortunately, the existence and survival and future of the church are in God's hands, not ours. Yet there is a sense in which we—by God's grace—must be sold on it and must sell it to others.

Members who are sold on their church's programs and activities and fellowship are much more likely to accept responsibilities of ownership and to uphold the church with their prayers, presence, gifts, and service.

Prospective members are more likely to join once they have been sold on what the church can do to help them meet their needs to belong and serve, and their needs to be comforted and inspired.

People in the community will be more supportive of the church when they are sold on it and confident that is not a private club for members only; when they understand that it is *for* the community as well as *in* the community; when they see that it is vitally interested in enriching the quality of their lives.

In 1913, Christian F. Reisner wrote a book entitled *Church Publicity*. He observed that the church "sometimes rocks itself to sleep with affirmations of its indispensability" and declared that the world must be made aware of what the church has to offer.[1]

In 1945, Stewart Harral, in *Public Relations for Churches,* reminded his generation that even though it had "many new activities and services, magnificent physical plants, and consecrated leadership, the church still has a selling problem of great magnitude." Many persons, he said, thought of the church as "an antiquated institution which appeals only to women and children, and really has little to offer in transforming the lives of people everywhere."[2]

The message these men of insight proclaimed to their generations needs to be proclaimed to ours: "The church must be sold."

It takes a team working together to sell a church. Generally, the pastor is the number one salesperson; however, secretaries, staff members, officers, Sunday school teachers, evangelism workers, ushers, newsletter editors, communications and public relations committee members, and leaders of various groups exert tremendous influence. In a sense, every member of the church—consciously or unconsciously—helps influence someone's opinion of the congregation, of the church in general, and of what it means to be a Christian.

Each chapter in this book offers suggestions to help clergy and laypersons solve problems (opportunities or obstacles) related to selling the church to members, prospective members, or the general public. The solutions are based on principles of communications and public relations that are effective in the marketplace *and* consistent with the teachings of Jesus.

I trust that God will use this book to help you sell your church to a world that desperately needs what God offers in and through the body of Christ.

CHAPTER 1

DISCOVERING A SENSE OF MISSION

Have you ever been intrigued by the sensational headlines on tabloid newspapers at grocery store check-out stands?

I have. In fact, I have a newspaper I bought in July 1987 because I couldn't resist the teaser across the top of page one: "COUPLE HIDES IN A BOMB SHELTER 25 YEARS."

The article says that in October 1962, a couple in Wetzler, Germany, Hermann Moller and his wife Helga (both 35 at the time), were convinced that the Cuban Missile Crisis would touch off an atomic war.

Hermann and Helga invested five million dollars in a bomb shelter and stocked the 570-square-foot underground room with enough food and provisions to last them until the twenty-first century.

Three days after they went into the bomb shelter, their radio went dead, says the article. The Mollers concluded that the world had been destroyed. They often talked about going outside, but were frightened about what had happened to the world and of what they might see. Since they had everything they needed to survive, they cautiously remained underground. Time lost its meaning.

In 1981, Helga had a heart attack and died. Hermann remained in the shelter until 1987, when, at age sixty, he opened the door and stepped outside. To his surprise, the world had not been destroyed.

The article quotes Moller as saying to reporters: "I lost twenty-five good years of my life for nothing."[1]

I cannot attest to the accuracy of the article, but I can attest to this: Countless people, terrified by world or personal crises, are looking for somewhere to hide. It's as though they want to dig a hole and bury themselves alive, just as the Mollers (allegedly) did.

It is not fear of the future that makes some people want to escape from the world. They are terrified, not by what may happen tomorrow, but by what did happen yesterday.

People don't fear monsters from outer space; they fear themselves. They have failed to live up to their own standards and to the expectations of people who are important to them.

Some think the best of life has passed them by. Many believe their lives are hopeless messes and have decided that since there's no way out, they might as well "live it up" until the curtain falls.

Many are weary of rushing at breakneck speed, not knowing or caring where they are going. Others know they are headed in the wrong direction and would like to turn around, but they don't know how.

People are discouraged, tired, and overburdened. They feel alone. They have no one to confide in, no one with whom to share their joys and sorrows.

Whether an individual is male or female, young or old, rich or poor, educated or uneducated, an astronaut or an accountant, he or she is a child of God and, consequently, has much in common with God's other children.

We all need inner strength to deal with fear and guilt and disappointment and despair and whatever else may threaten us. We need release from what is keeping us from being the best we can be, and we need the vision to see the tremendous potential that is always present.

The world has changed dramatically, even within the past few decades; but one thing has not changed: people still need to hear the good news Jesus Christ proclaimed to the world. Proclaiming it is our mission. We need to realize how much people need for us to do what God calls us to do.

Many industries that were growing rapidly a few years ago are in decline today, not because there's no need for what they have to offer, but because those who manage them have lost sight of what their industries have to offer. The same is true of churches.

In their book entitled *The Marketing Imagination,* Theodore Levitt, editor of the *Harvard Business Review,* and Edward W. Carter, professor of business administration, Harvard Business School, point out that railroads did not stop growing because the needs for passenger and freight transportation declined. Those needs grew. Railroads got in trouble because their managers assumed they were in the railroad business, rather than in the transportation business.[2]

Similarly, some churches are declining today, not because people no longer need what the church has to offer, but because those who manage the church have forgotten what the Christian gospel has to offer. Some of us think we are in church work, rather than in God's work.

Preoccupied with attracting new members, raising the budget, organizing the structure, and maintaining the machinery, we have lost sight of our real mission. We have focused so much time and energy on helping the church grow that we have forgotten what the church is called to be and do. We have neglected to nurture our own spirits and the spirits of others. We have been intrigued with "playing church" and have been mesmerized by power and position.

When the sons of Zebedee asked Jesus to appoint them to great positions, Jesus reminded them that true greatness is achieved, not by filling great positions, but by filling great needs. By washing the feet of his disciples,

Jesus demonstrated that he had come as a servant, "not to be served, but to serve, and to give his life a ransom for many" (Mark 10:45).

The church—as the body of the risen Christ—exists to serve. When it stops serving, it stops existing, even though it may appear to be thriving.

All over the nation, countless hundreds of churches of every size, theological persuasion, and denominational affiliation are focusing on serving. They are aware of their main business, and they know they are agents through whom Jesus works. They know their task is to preach good news to the poor, to proclaim release to the captive and recovery of sight to the blind, to set at liberty those who are oppressed, and to proclaim the acceptable year of the Lord.

Churches that are pursuing their mission don't always make the news, but they do always make a difference. They come in all sizes, in a wide variety of settings, and wear many different denominational labels. What follows are a few examples of what some Episcopal churches are doing.

In Atlanta, St Luke's Episcopal Church has a community kitchen that feeds five hundred homeless persons each weekday, a street academy that offers education for students needing help, a job placement and counseling service for the homeless, and a clinic that supplied medical services in 1989 for 16,000 homeless people.

In Los Angeles, the Church and Temple Housing Corporation, a joint venture of three Episcopal churches, renovated several hotels, thus enabling skid row residents to move from flophouses into safe, warm, modern rooms with shared kitchens and baths. Tenants may join in potluck meals, Bible studies, recreational outings, and friendship groups.

At Trinity Episcopal Church in New Orleans, affordable mental-health care is available through expanded pastoral counseling. Professional therapists donate their time.

In Baltimore, the Church of the Resurrection has opened "Noah's Ark," a day-care center.

I recently talked with an 82-year-old man who has been a member of the same church since childhood. He said that the church has always been a vital part of his life, that the church taught him the values he lives by, that it gives him a place to serve others, and that it sustains him during good times and bad.

"I've had my church to cling to," he said, "and it has never let me down."

Thousands of men and women all over the world tell the same story: "I've had my church to cling to, and it has never let me down." Our mission is to provide people with something to cling to that will always sustain them.

CHAPTER 2

FINDING A NEW IDENTITY

Viktor Frankl gained profound insights into human behavior during World War II, while he was a prisoner at Auschwitz and other Nazi concentration camps.

Like thousands of other prisoners, he experienced hunger, cold, and brutality. The danger of death loomed night and day. All prisoners were subjected to the same barbaric treatment, but Frankl observed that all did not respond the same way.

In his book *Man's Search for Meaning,* Frankl reflects upon what made the difference in how people responded. He writes: "Woe to him who saw no more sense in his life, no aim, no purpose, and therefore no point in carrying on. He was soon lost."[1]

That same observation applies to churches. Woe to the congregation that has no aim, no purpose, and therefore no point in carrying on. It is lost.

Members who are convinced that God has a mission for their church are "sold on the church." They are proud of it. They cheerfully support it to the point of sacrifice. They don't give up in tough times.

From the days of St. Paul to our days, churches with a reason for being have thrived, even under oppressive conditions. A church that has a reason to live finds a way to live.

How do we discover a reason to live? By finding a new identity; by realizing who we are and whose we are. How do we do that? By answering this basic question: "What does God want to accomplish in and through us?"

The following case study shows how one church found its reason for being.

A Case Study: St. Andrew's United Methodist Church

On a Sunday afternoon in January 1955, two hundred people gathered on a hill in northeast Oklahoma City to break ground for a new Methodist church.

Even though St. Andrew's was named in honor of Simon Peter's brother—the patron saint of ordinary people—the charter members were confident that their church would not be ordinary. They were right.

Times were booming in Oklahoma City, and the new church was located in one of the city's fastest growing areas. On groundbreaking day, twenty-

Finding a New Identity

one new homes within five blocks of the church were near completion. Young families were moving to the area, and children were everywhere.

St. Andrew's grew rapidly. Within five years, the church had nearly one thousand members. Ground was broken again—this time for a two-story education building with a big fellowship hall. When it was completed, church leaders drew plans and started raising funds for a sanctuary that would seat eight hundred. It appeared they were going to need it.

Times changed abruptly. During the early 1960s, the neighborhood around St. Andrew's experienced what many neighborhoods across the nation experienced in that decade: "white flight." Most members of the church moved out of the neighborhood and joined churches near their new homes.

In 1973, I was appointed pastor of St. Andrew's. My wife, Arlene, and I and our two daughters—Melody, six, and Gina, four—moved into the parsonage a few blocks from the church. We were the only white family within several blocks. Melody and Gina attended the neighborhood public school, which was ninety-six percent black.

St. Andrew's still had more than five hundred people on the church roll, but attendance was down to fifty. Most active members lived about three miles away.

Ken Jones, pastor of Trinity United Methodist Church in Atlanta, visited St. Andrew's one weekend to help us develop a strategy for ministry. He challenged us to grapple with basic questions: What do people in this neighborhood need? What resources has God given us that might help them? What does God want to accomplish through us?

We had been asking such questions as, "What are we going to do if we have to buy a new furnace?" Now we were asking, "How can we help spread God's warmth in this fragmented neighborhood? How can we help improve the quality of life for people who have had to settle far too long with far too little?"

Frankly, we didn't know what people's needs were or how we could help, but we knew how to find out. We asked ten key leaders in the neighborhood to attend a meeting at the church. We assured them that we were not going to lecture, but that we were going to listen to them as they told us their concerns and interests. We asked them to be candid; we promised to take them seriously. In public relations terms, we held a "focus group."

While the community leaders spoke, we listed the neighborhood needs they said were the most crucial. They said that students in the elementary school needed special help with reading and math; teenagers needed a place for recreation; adults—especially single parents—needed help with child care and stimulating activities to enrich their lives socially and intellectually.

Several leaders expressed concern about aging parents—some of whom were in a nearby nursing home.

During our next planning session, we examined the list of neighborhood needs and began to brainstorm about how the congregation could help meet those needs.

One resource we had to offer the community was our building. We had ten classrooms that were being used solely for the storage of discarded furniture and equipment. We opened some of that space for a day-care center. We made another room available for a counseling center for low-income families.

The greatest resources we had to offer the community were our gifted members, who had a rare combination of talent and eagerness to be involved in meaningful service.

One member, who had a doctorate in special education, designed an after-school tutoring program for students from the neighborhood elementary school. On the first day of the program, the school bus delivered about forty children to our church.

To provide the personalized instruction that the children needed, we recruited retired school teachers and others who were willing and able to teach. Not only did we provide tutoring and snacks, we provided a safe and pleasant place for the children to be after school.

To help provide recreation for teenagers, we put up basketball goals in our parking lot. Our youth director organized activities for a neighborhood recreation night. We cleaned out a log building and turned it into a home for the two scout troops that we sponsored.

My wife and an energetic 80-year-old member developed a singing group for children of the church and community. Another member—a retired school teacher—started a story time for neighborhood youngsters.

One of our members—a professor of anatomical science at the University of Oklahoma Medical School—taught classes to help people understand the aging process and other health issues.

Another member—an insurance underwriter—developed a personalized ministry to senior adults and persons with handicapping conditions. He counseled people who were in financial trouble and was an advocate for anyone who was being exploited.

Two of our members took literacy training and helped adults in the neighborhood learn to read.

In response to the need for stimulating educational opportunities for adults, we developed continuing education classes. To let people know about the classes, we mailed flyers to every home within two miles of the church. Our attendance the first night was seventy-five, and it grew.

Finding a New Identity

Black people might not have been ready to worship in a white church on Sunday morning, but they were ready to come on Tuesday night to learn arts and crafts and to pursue other studies. Before that first eight-week session was over, students were asking for more advanced classes and for classes in other subjects, including gardening, photography, first aid, and money management.

Incidentally, white people were not doing all the teaching. It was inspiring to see a group of white women gathered around a black woman who taught them needlepoint and other crafts.

One afternoon, after our neighborhood ministries had been underway for about three years, a teenager who lived down the street stopped by my office. "Rev. Bowdon," he said, "I can show you how people used to break into this church."

He led me around to the side of the building. We stopped at the door. He took out his pocketknife, pushed the blade between the door and the doorjamb, and opened the lock in a matter of seconds.

"That's how they used to do it," he said, "but they won't do it any more. We won't let them."

I'll never forget that experience! Burglaries had been a problem for us and for other churches in the area. In fact, one nearby church had bought an attack dog and turned him loose inside the building to "protect it" against neighborhood kids. The kids got the message and stayed away. However, by protecting itself, the church practically killed itself, as is usually the case for churches and for people.

The teenager's comment was significant to me because it assured me that we were winning the trust of people in the neighborhood. For a while they had been suspicious, and they had a right to be in view of what they had previously experienced. But as trust grew, St. Andrew's became their church.

It would be misleading to imply that everything we tried at St. Andrew's worked. Most of our ideas failed to produce all that we had hoped. We remembered that programs are not sacred. If they didn't work, or if they quit working, we junked them.

It would also be misleading to imply that as soon as we started focusing on service rather than survival, we solved all our problems. We still had problems, but we did make progress. By October 1978, when I was appointed pastor of another church, St. Andrew's was averaging 125 in worship.

After I left, the people of St. Andrew's continued to put service ahead of survival. In fact, in 1980, the congregation decided that their greatest service would be to disband as a congregation and turn their building over to Quayle United Methodist Church, a neighboring black congregation that critically needed a better building and location.

The change brought new life to Quayle. From 1980 to 1990, membership grew from 150 to 225. Quayle is now the strongest minority church in the Oklahoma Conference of The United Methodist Church.

What happened to the members of St. Andrew's? Some joined Quayle: one is now the congregation's lay leader. Several families transferred to a small church in a nearby transitional neighborhood. Across the years, they have helped it become a dynamic church that has no racial barriers. Other members of St. Andrew's now serve in key leadership positions in at least six other churches.

REFLECTIONS

The St. Andrew's case study illustrates that too much "navel gazing" doesn't help churches or people.

A church does not find its identity by grieving about lost glory and greatness, by fretting about its frailties, or by dreading disasters that might strike.

A church finds itself the same way a person finds himself or herself—by focusing on the needs of others and by striving to be an instrument though whom God meets needs.

CHAPTER 3

Empowering Lay Ministry

During the summer of 1989, Vincent Capretta of Cleveland mailed 1.2 million letters soliciting funds for the St. Anthony Friary. In response, concerned citizens sent him more than $300,000. There was a problem, however: the friary did not exist. Capretta used the money to support his singing career. He was convicted on thirty-two counts of mail fraud.

What does this story illustrate? Obviously, it shows that some people are untrustworthy and others are too trusting, but it also demonstrates that many people want to share what they have. They want to be involved in causes they believe will make life better for others. It is a shame that compassionate people are sometimes exploited.

It is also a shame that the church often fails to provide opportunities for members to be involved in significant and fulfilling ministries.

In far too many churches, laypeople think of themselves as spectators. They come on Sunday to hear the preacher and the choir and to consume what they think will help them get through the week. They pitch a few dollars in the collection plate and conclude that they have done their part. Unfortunately, some clergy also view laypeople as benefactors and consumers of ministry, rather than as people through whom God ministers.

WHY EMPOWER LAYPEOPLE FOR MINISTRY?

Here are some good reasons for empowering laypeople for ministry.
- Jesus set the standard for empowering laypeople for ministry. Mary Magdalene, a social outcast, and Simon, a flighty fisherman, were among the many ordinary people through whom Jesus accomplished extraordinary results.
- Ministry was the way of life for early Christians. The Apostle Paul believed his task as a servant of God was to "equip saints for the work of ministry." In the early church, a few individuals were enlisted to provide leadership, vision, and perspective; but their primary job was to help the people of God "do ministry."
- Baptism is ordination into the priesthood of believers. As Martin Luther pointed out five hundred years ago, professional clergy do not have exclusive rights or total reponsibility for ministry.
- God calls laypeople to be on the front lines of life, using their training, experience, skills, and insights to enrich the lives of others.

- Laypeople who lose themselves in servanthood find fulfillment and grow spiritually.
- Churches that provide meaningful opportunities for laypeople to minister tend to grow in membership and in influence.
- Few churches can hire enough people to do all the work that needs to be done.

HOW IS LAY MINISTRY DEVELOPED?

Appointing people to committees and getting them involved in the machinery of the church is not all it takes to develop lay ministry. What does it take? Church of the Servant (United Methodist) in Oklahoma City has an answer.

Even though the congregation has more than 3,500 members, only 11 laypeople serve on the administrative board. However, more than 1,500 serve in specific lay ministries.

The Rev. Norman Neaves, the founding pastor of Church of the Servant, admits it took him a few years to discover the importance of involving laypeople in ministry.

The church began in June 1968 with one member, Neaves's wife, Kip. He spent the summer knocking on doors in the neighborhood, looking for people who might want to help start a new Methodist congregation.

At the first worship service in September 1968, some 148 people joined the church. By January 1969, membership had jumped to 302. Every year since then, membership has grown by several hundred.

Obviously, the pastor's job grew as the church grew. Within five years, Neaves was doing thirty-two hours of counseling a week. He was constantly on the run, making calls at hospitals scattered over the metropolitan area.

"I wasn't very bright to be committing to such a heavy schedule," he admits. "I was running myself ragged. Begrudgingly, I had to come to terms with sharing the leadership of the church. I had gotten so many strokes for doing it by myself that I didn't want to share the limelight. However, I knew I couldn't continue that way."

In 1973, Church of the Servant hired the Rev. Bob Gardenhire as minister of pastoral care. His primary function was to visit hospitals.

At first, having Gardenhire make hospital calls didn't solve the problem, even though he was clinically trained and an ordained minister. People were happy for him to visit; but more often than not, when he was getting ready to leave, they would ask, "When is Norman coming?" In effect, they were saying, "We appreciate your coming by, but it doesn't count until Norman comes by, because he's my minister."

After a few months, Gardenhire's ministry was established in its own right. However, by then it was evident the two pastors could not provide enough care. Moreover, the needs for pastoral care were so great that the church could not hire enough people to do the ministries.

With his clinical training as a supervisor in pastoral care, Gardenhire began to train a group of laypeople to deliver hospital ministry. He recruited eight people and worked with them for a year. In weekly retreats, he taught them how to listen, speak, pray, share the faith, and understand the hospital setting and the meaning of illness and crisis.

When the laypeople completed training and began their ministry in the hospitals, Neaves and Gardenhire reduced their visitation roles considerably. One pastor visited the hospitals every third day and was there when members had surgery, but lay ministers did the hospital ministry the rest of the time. Before long, a second team of eight lay ministers was brought into being; then a third team of eight; then a fourth.

Today, Church of the Servant has twenty-five or thirty people in the hospital at any given time. Yet Neaves, as senior pastor, visits hospitals only four or five times a year. Gardenhire visits four or five times a week, calling on people who are having surgery. All other hospital calls are made by lay ministers of care.

Neaves admits that during the early days of his ministry he would have considered what his church is now doing to be "completely harebrained and radical," but he is convinced this approach to ministry provides quality care to about six hundred patients and families a year.

After discovering how effective lay ministers could be, the Church of the Servant began using laypeople in other areas. Neaves and Gardenhire had been offering thirty to forty hours of counseling a week, and the load was more than they could handle. After discovering that the church had several members who were social workers, psychiatrists, clinical psychologists, and therapists, they decided to equip these laypeople theologically to be involved in counseling ministries.

In addition to those with professional training, the church had other members who possessed intuition and skills for helping people in trouble. With training, they could do an acceptable job of empathic listening, as long as they knew their boundaries and didn't overstep them. A team of lay counselors was brought into being and trained.

One of the lay counselors was the vice president of an oil company when he first became involved in Church of the Servant's care ministries. While making rounds at the hospital one day, he visited a terminally ill patient. The left side of her face had been eaten by cancer. She had no relatives or friends to visit her. The counselor began going to see her during his lunch hour, early in the morning before he went to work, and after work before he went home. Before long, he was visiting other terminally ill patients who had no one to stand by them. He got caught up in the ministry. When an opportunity developed for him to take early retirement from the oil company, he retired—even though he was still in his early fifties—so he could spend more time visiting the terminally ill. He is now working with eight patients who are dying.

Not long ago a woman he visited said she wanted him to do her funeral. He did so, with a little assistance from Neaves. "That story is replicated many times over," says Neaves. "That kind of bonding—that kind of care and love—is a beautiful and powerful thing for our laypeople to experience."

LAY MINISTERS PERFORM VARIED MINISTRIES

For people who don't want to get involved in issues of death and dying and for those who would feel out of place making evangelistic calls, teaching Sunday school, working with youth, or singing in the choir, the Church of the Servant has other opportunities for ministry.

About fifty people make up a building care team. "Our building has 35,000 square feet, and it is used by over two thousand people during the week, not including activities on Sunday," says Neaves. "We have only one full-time and one part-time custodian. However, we have volunteers who paint, clean carpets, fix plumbing, and build cabinets. They offer these skills as their ministry."

Church of the Servant also has "minute ministries" for people who want to help the church but cannot make major commitments of time. Their ministries might involve caring for plants in the church building, filling glue bottles for vacation church school, or working at a church carnival.

LAY MINISTERS ENTER COVENANTS

Many people who are involved in lay ministries at Church of the Servant—especially those with assignments that extend beyond three months— enter into covenants with the church. No covenant is for more than one year, but covenants may be renewed.

Church of the Servant sets forth objectives for each lay ministry to specify to laypeople what the church hopes will happen as a result of ministry efforts.

Laypersons are also asked to consider how they will benefit from their involvement in ministry. Neaves explains: "If you can't see how you will benefit, then you are not more than a step away from paternalism and a condescending kind of ministry. We don't feel that ministry happens with that kind of posture. Ministry happens when it is mutually shared."

Church of the Servant assures laypersons that they will be provided with training and resources to perform their tasks well. "You are not going to be out there all by yourself, paddling hard trying to make it," Neaves says. "We will be in the boat with you, doing our part."

Empowering Lay Ministry

Members who are involved in lay ministries bond with one another and with the church. "It gives power and excitement and integrity to everything else that we do as a congregation," Neaves says.

"I feel a deep sense of accomplishment when I can see the glow on the face of someone who helped a couple through a crisis over a six-month period or who helped a suicidal teenager get a handle on her life. It brings me a vicarious sense of fulfillment, knowing I am part of a community of faith that is empowering this kind of rich experience in ministry."

Neaves believes God endows every congregation with far more ministry than it can meet. "God has already implanted the seeds and the gifts for a phenomenal ministry. It is a matter of finding a way to call forth those gifts."

Finding a way to call forth people's gifts, obviously, requires good communication—clergy and laity must be in dialogue, listening to each other as well as talking.

Neaves encourages other churches to empower laity for ministry. Empowering laypeople for ministry, he says, helps everyone: the church, the pastor and professional staff, the people who are served, and the laypeople who are serving.

When pastors and other church leaders ask Neaves how to empower laypeople, he gives them the following ten suggestions:

1. Begin with the assumption that every person is a gift and bears a gift to the world.

2. Create a climate of affirmation and encouragement throughout the congregation.

3. Appreciate diversity. Don't make everyone squeeze into the same mold.

4. Help people see that their gifts and their ministries lie in their wants, not in their oughts.

5. Challenge people to have big dreams.

6. Focus on the future, not on the past. To call people forth, you must call them forward.

7. Encourage people to broaden their concept of ministry and their understanding of salvation as wholeness or completeness.

8. Be open to God's surprises. Something that might not seem like a ministry at first may turn out to be the greatest ministry your church will ever have.

9. Encourage laypeople to do their own thinking. Let others know that God is for them and that they can be and do what they were meant to be and do.

10. Get out of the way and give others a chance to shine.

CHAPTER 4

BUILDING POSITIVE RESPONSE WITH PR

A daily newspaper editor and I were visiting in his office one Saturday afternoon.

"Take a look at this," he said, pointing to the church page in his weekend edition that had just come off the press.

"We pulled two-thirds of these articles from the wire. Why did we use them? Simply because we didn't have enough local stories to fill the space. Churches in our town are doing lots of great things that would be interesting to readers, and we would be glad to run articles about them if somebody would send us news releases or fact sheets or just give us a call."

The editor's primary concern, however, was not with churches that neglected opportunities to use daily newspapers to reach the public with their messages. "The biggest need right now at my church is for improving internal communication, not external," he said.

"We have more than a thousand members. People can go to our church five years and not know five people, especially if they are not in a Sunday school class or some other small group. We have dozens of organizations, but they don't communicate with one another. How can we expect our members to be excited about the good things that are happening in our church if they don't know what is happening? How can we expect them to support the budget if they don't understand how it is used? Our people need to know what's going on and why."

The editor made his point. If we expect people to remain "sold on the church," if we expect them to support it with their time, talent, and tithes, then we must keep them informed about what the church is doing and why. This is "The Information Age." People expect to be informed. Laying guilt on them doesn't motivate them to be cheerful givers.

Church members are constantly receiving appeals from worthy causes, but they can't help everybody. Churches have to compete for support. How can churches compete? One way is by using the public relations principles and procedures that are effective in the marketplace.

As church leaders, we need to learn all we can from public relations professionals, just as we need to learn all we can from professional educators, counselors, business administrators, and other specialists who have expertise that can help advance the mission and ministry of the church.

Building Positive Response with PR

"Now just a minute," you may be saying. "Don't tell me the church should resort to PR gimmicks to proclaim the gospel of Jesus Christ!"

I can understand such a response. In fact, when I left the pastorate in 1981 to become director of communications and public relations for the Oklahoma Conference of The United Methodist Church, I was disturbed by the public relations part of my title. I thought of myself as a minister, not as a "snake-oil salesman."

Like many other people, when I heard the term "public relations," I immediately thought of cover-ups and build-ups and ballyhoo. But after working for a decade with public relations professionals, I have high respect and appreciation for their insights and skills.

I think Stewart Harral, professor at the University of Oklahoma, was right when he made this observation:

> "Public relations does not constitute a panacea for all the problems confronting pastors and churches, but when rightly used and intelligently directed, it can aid immeasurably in gaining favorable acceptance, building good will, and securing support and co-operation for the church."[1]

Public relations can help us "make friends for Christ and his church," which is how Ralph Stoody—a pioneer in the field of religious public relations and author of a book on the subject—once described the purpose of church public relations.

Because of misconceptions about this often-maligned profession, we need to take a fresh look at PR so we can make the best possible use of public relations principles and procedures.

What Is Public Relations?

Scott Cutlip and Allen H. Center, in their textbook *Effective Public Relations,* offer the following definition:

> "Public relations is the planned effort to influence opinion through good character and responsible performance, based upon mutually satisfactory two-way communication."[2]

As this definition states, the purpose of public relations is to influence opinion. Based on the assumption that opinions influence action, public relations practitioners seek to reinforce favorable opinions, sway neutral opinions, and remedy unfavorable opinions, thereby producing positive perceptions and positive reponses. We could say that "PR" stands for "positive response." Positive response, of course, is what we are seeking in the church.

CHARACTER AND PERFORMANCE MATTER MOST

Even though public relations professionals are in the image-making business, they know that the campaigns they design and implement will not be effective long unless they are backed by the integrity and performance of the client.

As Cutlip and Center state in their definition, effective public relations requires good character and responsible performance. Images may be fashioned by advertising, but they must be sustained by performance.

Jesus emphasized the importance of good character and responsible performance when he said, "A good tree cannot bear bad fruit, nor can a bad tree bear good fruit" (Matthew 7:18).

The emphasis that public relations professionals place on character and performance should remind clergy and laity that ability is no substitute for good character and responsible performance. A pastor may be powerful in the pulpit and brilliant in board meetings, but will accomplish little if he or she is aloof in the shopping mall. Members want to know that the pastor cares about them.

A church cannot sustain the image of being warm and caring if the people and the pastor are cold and indifferent. A church can put billboards at every major intersection, place full-page ads in the Sunday paper, and run TV and radio spots at prime time on every station in the market; it can have manicured lawns, beautiful buildings, plenty of parking, and every comfort and convenience money can buy, but if people come to the church and feel like intruders; if they sense that nobody cares whether or not they come back; if they leave without being comforted or challenged by the gospel, they are not likely to return.

The compassion Jesus showed to people who were in trouble and the courage he showed when he was in trouble proved to be the clearest disclosures ever given of God's love and the best examples ever given of good character and responsible performance.

COMMUNICATION IS VITAL

Cutlip and Center say that the other essential ingredient for influencing people is "mutually satisfactory two-way communication."

In a sense, it's redundant to say "two-way communication," because all genuine communication is two-way—consisting of listening as well as speaking.

Jesus was aware of the importance of two-way communication. He never wrote a book or anything else—as far as we know—except for the few words he scribbled in the dust the day he was asked to prescribe punishment for a woman caught in adultery. However, Jesus had a simple and memorable way of expressing profound truth.

Like other effective communicators, Jesus was a great listener. The Samaritan woman Jesus visited at the well in Jericho discovered that Jesus not only heard what she was saying, but that he heard what she was not saying. She knew he understood her; and because he understood her, she understood herself better.

You may be a captivating and informing speaker, you may win awards for oratory; but if you can't hear what others are saying, you are not a good communicator.

In the local church, effective communication involves more than inspiring preaching and informative newsletters. A church that communicates with its people knows where they hurt, what they hope for, and what they think.

Here are two examples of how listening pays off:

- In 1989, when the movie *The Last Temptation of Christ* was in the news, a Presbyterian pastor in Dayton listened to the controversy and identified a problem. To deal with the problem, he purchased ads referring to the film and announcing that he was leading a Sunday school class on the nature of Jesus Christ.

  Local newspapers and radio and television stations reported what he was doing. Forty people came into the church who had never been there before, simply because the pastor was able to take a problem and turn it around. He said, "Look, we have the story about Jesus Christ. We can provide a way to learn more about him." This opportunity would never have arisen if the pastor had not been listening.

- Good listening helped an Episcopal priest in Pittsburg discover why few young adults attended Sunday morning worship, even though many attended the Thursday night program. By listening, he learned that many young adults worked on Sunday morning. He started a Sunday evening service, and attendance picked up dramatically.

When we listen to others, we often learn something that helps us. In addition, when we listen to others, they are far more likely to listen to us and to respond positively to our message. Public relations professionals have refined several effective methods that can help church leaders listen to members, prospective members, and others. The methods include surveys, questionnaires, focus groups, and in-depth interviews.

THE PUBLIC INCLUDES MANY PUBLICS

Public relations professionals remind us that even though people aren't all the same, they have certain characteristics and concerns in common, such as age, educational background, financial position, attitudes, values, or interests. Public relations people refer to each group as a "public."

Jesus knew that he had a variety of publics. Those for him made up one public; those against him made up another. Each of those publics could be subdivided into dozens of other publics.

The church has a variety of publics, too. The church has an internal public (members) and an external public (non-members). The internal public might be divided into several publics—active, inactive, resident, and non-resident members. Each of these might be divided further. Similarly, the external public might be divided into prospects and non-prospects; and those publics could in turn be subdivided into smaller publics.

TARGET YOUR MARKET

What appeals to one public may not appeal to another. A communications method that reaches one public may not reach another. Wise communicators not only know their subject, they know their publics and address them appropriately by focusing on concerns, needs, and interests. This procedure is called "targeting the market."

Jesus was a master at targeting his market. He understood people and cared deeply for them. When speaking to farmers, he talked about sowing and reaping; when speaking to fishermen, he talked about nets and fishing and being "fishers of men."

Following the example that Jesus set, the writers of Matthew, Mark, Luke, and John kept their audiences and objectives in mind when writing.

Great communicators of the Christian faith have targeted their markets. Martin Luther—a leader of the Protestant Reformation—is an example. When translating the Bible from the original tongues into idiomatic German, he was determined to "make Moses so German that no one would ever suspect he was a Jew."

In a tract he wrote in 1503, Luther reported that he sometimes spent three or four weeks searching for a single word, and he sometimes scarcely finished three lines in four days. He went to incredible pains to find the exact German word to convey the true meaning of the original passage. While searching for a word to describe a precious stone in Revelation 21, he examined the court jewels of Frederick the Wise. To describe the sacrifices that are reported in Leviticus, he needed terms for the internal parts of goats and bullocks, so he went to a slaughterhouse and asked the butcher about the parts in question.

Another Christian communicator who targeted his market was John Wesley, one of the founders of the Methodist Church. When preaching in a cathedral to a congregation of scholars, Wesley preached in a learned style; but when standing on a cart outside a coal mine preaching to workers, he adjusted his language and style of delivery.

"I design plain truth for plain people," Wesley wrote in the preface to the first volume of his collected edition of *Sermons on Several Occasions*, published in 1746.

"Therefore, of set purpose, I abstain from all nice and philosophical speculations; from all perplexed and intricate reasonings; and, as far as possible, from even the show of learning, unless in sometimes citing original Scripture. I labour to avoid all words which are not easy to be understood, all which are not used in common life; and, in particular, those kinds of technical terms that so frequently occur in Bodies of Divinity; those modes of speaking which men of reading are intimately acquainted with, but which to common people are an unknown tongue. Yet I am not assured, that I do not sometimes slide into them unawares: It is so extremely natural to imagine, that a word which is familiar to ourselves is so to all the world."[3]

Read Wesley's sermons, and you will agree that he did sometimes "slide unawares" not only into an unknown tongue, but into perplexing and intricate reasonings. However, scholars say the published sermons are not transcriptions of sermons Wesley preached. They were aimed at a different audience and designed for a different purpose.

Wesley wrote a variety of tracts that were designed to speak to specific groups, including drunkards, swearers, sabbath-breakers, street-walkers, and condemned malefactors awaiting the hangman's noose.[4]

Developing an Ongoing PR Program

Contrary to commonly-held views, public relations is not a knee-jerk reaction to a crisis, a scheme to smooth over a scandal, a cover-up to calm a crowd, or a scam to raise money.

Cutlip and Center state in their definition that public relations is *a planned effort* that involves research—listening; planning—decision making; communication—action; and evaluation.[5]

FORM A COMMITTEE

Committees are not the answer to the world's problems. If they were, all our problems would be solved. However, sometimes committees are essential.

The public relations task calls for a committee. It cannot be completed adequately by one person, regardless of how talented that person might be. The task is too comprehensive and too vital to be taken lightly. It demands and deserves a team effort.

It doesn't matter what the church public relations committee is called; what does matter is that its job is done well. The committee should include good communicators who are "sold on the church" and are committed to selling it to others.

PREPARE A PROFILE OF YOUR CHURCH

"Before you execute, or even plan, you must understand. And the first step in understanding consists of knowing yourself," Robert T. Reilly observes in *Public Relations in Action.*[6]

In keeping with Reilly's advice, the first assignment for a church public relations committee is to "know the church." Before committee members write press releases or design promotional pieces, they need to look and listen. The more they know about the church and what it has to offer, the better they will be able to sell it.

Two worksheets are found at the end of this chapter. Each has a distinctive purpose. *Worksheet A: Profile of Our Church* will guide the public relations committee in doing research and listening. Completing it may take several weeks. Make this a churchwide effort. Enlist people of different ages and interests to assist. The public relations committee should work closely with other committees that have related interests.

The information that is gathered will be invaluable to the public relations committee when it begins producing promotional resources. In addition, the information will help programming and administrative bodies of the church identify needs and develop ministries to meet the needs. Much of the information will interest the total congregation.

After the profile has been prepared, the public relations committee should focus on sharing the findings.

Worksheet B: Church Public Relations Project will help the public relations committee ask the right questions and gather the basic information it needs to design and develop public relations campaigns for specific projects.

Worksheet A:

Profile of Our Church

1. Determine how people in today's society feel about religion and about the church in general. Skim magazines and books. See *It's A Different World* by Lyle Schaller (Abingdon Press, 1987) and *The People's Religion: American Faith in the 90's* by George Gallup and Jim Castelli (Macmillan, 1990).

2. Prepare a history (not more than 1,000 words) of your church.

3. Review church records for at least five years and determine changes in membership, worship attendance, Sunday school attendance, and church finances. Prepare a chart presenting this information.

4. On a map of the community that your church serves, use markers or pens of different colors to mark the following: the location of your church building; homes of members who have belonged to the church for more than three years; homes of members who have joined within the past five years.

5. Study the neighborhood where the church is located. Note changes within the past five years in population, racial makeup, economy, housing, commercial and industrial development, traffic patterns, schools, medical services, and other items that may have an impact upon the church. For information, consult neighborhood schools, local libraries, utility companies, or the chamber of commerce. Prepare a report on your findings.

6. List changes that are likely to occur in the community within the next five or ten years and speculate about how the changes may influence your church. Also consider how your church can help bring about progress in the community. The city planning commission or chamber of commerce can probably help.

7. Identify six of your church's major publics.

8. Review the relationship that the church has with each of the major publics identified in item 7. Listen to what people within the publics say; try to understand their values and attitudes; be sensitive to their interests, needs, and concerns. Here are some suggestions:

- Do individual interviews with a few representatives of the church's various publics.

- Bring together focus groups representing different publics and give them opportunities to express opinions and offer suggestions.
- Mail a questionnaire—such as the following—to all members of the church, or at least to a cross section. Ask members to return the questionnaire, unsigned, within a week. Enclose a self-addressed, stamped envelope if your budget permits.

HOW ARE WE DOING?

Do you feel that our church is ministering effectively to the needs of:

Children?	____ Usually	____ Often	____ Seldom
Youth?	____ Usually	____ Often	____ Seldom
Young adults?	____ Usually	____ Often	____ Seldom
Middle adults?	____ Usually	____ Often	____ Seldom
Older adults?	____ Usually	____ Often	____ Seldom
Singles?	____ Usually	____ Often	____ Seldom
Families?	____ Usually	____ Often	____ Seldom

What more would you like to see our church do. *Write on the back.*

Worksheet B:

Church Public Relations Project

Name of Project: _____ Date: _____

1. What do you want to accomplish with this project?

   Primary objective: _____

   Secondary objective: _____

2. If your objectives are accomplished, how will the mission of your church be advanced?

   _____

   _____

3. What is unique or appealing about the program or proposal you offer?

   _____

   _____

4. What is the central message you wish to communicate? State it in 25 or fewer words.

   _____

   _____

5. What three groups do you hope to reach with your message? How can each group benefit from what you have to offer in this project?

   Group: _____ Potential Benefit: _____

   Group: _____ Potential Benefit: _____

   Group: _____ Potential Benefit: _____

6. What is your budget for this project? _____
7. What is the deadline for completing this project: _____
8. Give the names and phone numbers of two resource persons who can assist in this project.

   Name: _____ Phone Number: _____

   Name: _____ Phone Number: _____

9. In view of your objective, your target audiences, your budget, and your deadline, what means of communication will best convey your message?

☐ Brochure ☐ Newsletter   ☐ Direct Mail

☐ Videotape ☐ Multimedia Presentation ☐ Press Releases

☐ Other: _____

COMMUNICATION GUIDE

1. What do you want to say?

2. To whom do you want to say it?

3. Why do you want to say it? What response do you want?

4. What communication media will enable you to say it best?

CHAPTER 5

Prospecting for Members

How important is religion to Americans? A Gallup study researched that question in 1988 for a coalition of twenty-two religious groups. Fifty-four percent of those questioned said religion was "very important" in their lives; thirty-two percent said it was "fairly important"; and fourteen percent said it was "not very important."[1]

According to Gallup, sixty-five percent of Americans identified themselves as members of a church or synagogue in 1988—the lowest percentage since the Gallup Poll began tracking such figures in 1937.[2]

What insights can we glean from these studies? One conclusion we might draw is that churches have a lot of prospects. People who recognize the importance of religion in their lives but don't go to church are like people who recognize the importance of education but don't go to school. Many are prime prospects for the church. Studies by Gallup also indicate that some people don't attend church simply because they haven't been asked.

However, recruitment of new members is not simple. We need to look beneath the surface. Why do people who recognize the importance of religion choose not to be part of a church?

Gallup concludes that Americans are increasingly divorcing their personal religious behavior from their attitudes toward organized religion. "They view their religion as a relationship between themselves and God: organized religion is an important part of that relationship. But if organized religion fails to live up to their expectations, Americans will hold it in less esteem—but they won't let that lowered esteem affect their own behavior."[3]

Americans became more critical of their churches and synagogues during the 1980s. "A large majority believes the churches are too concerned with internal organizational issues and not sufficiently concerned with spiritual matters."[4]

To reach people who don't go to church but who recognize the importance of religion, clergy and laypersons must demonstrate genuine concern for people and present convincing evidence that their church can contribute to the development of people's faith in God. We must offer people something they want if we expect them to join the church and support it with their time, talent, and tithes.

Jarrell Tyson, a United Methodist church growth specialist who consults with churches all over the country, says people don't attend church for one of two reasons: "Either the church is not ministering to their needs, or they are unaware that the church can minister to their needs."

Let's consider some ways clergy and laypersons can let prospects know they are missing something if they are not active in a church.

Telemarketing

You and your spouse are having a quiet dinner at home. The phone rings. Fearing the call is from a loved one who is in trouble, you rush to answer it.

The voice you hear is not that of a loved one, or of anyone for that matter. Your caller is a computer that says you have won a fabulous prize, if you can answer a simple question.

In disgust, you place the receiver on the hook—or you leave it off to avoid another computer-generated call.

Why do so many businesses use telemarketing? Because they have found that it helps them find prospects quickly and at a fairly low cost.

Like it or not, one of the best ways to develop a prospect list is to use the phone. True, some businesses annoy us with their abuse of telemarketing, but that is no reason for the church not to use the phone in a responsible manner.

Some churches have come into being as a result of telemarketing, as we shall see in the following case study.

The Rev. Morgan Wallace arrived in Lawrenceville, a suburb of Atlanta, on August 1, 1989, to establish Peace Presbyterian Church. He rented space in a twelve-screen-theater in a new shopping center. To find prospective members, Wallace used a method that several other Cumberland Presbyterian churches had used with considerable success: "Phone for You."

Obviously, prospecting by phone requires many callers. Usually, callers are recruited from other churches in the area. Since there were no other Cumberland Presbyterian churches in Atlanta, Wallace asked Presbyterians in other areas to help. They did. A total of 160 from several states agreed to call prospects long-distance.

One of the first steps Wallace took in training callers was to help them have a positive attitude toward making "cold calls" on the phone.

"Since the word 'telemarketing' has negative connotations for many people, we changed the terminology to 'Personal Contacts by Phone.' This helped our callers keep from feeling they were being asked to sell God."

During orientation, callers were assured that they were not alone, that God was at work.

"We assured our callers that the people God wanted us to touch would respond favorably. This strengthened their confidence. 'What's important,' we said, 'is to be genuine and warm and caring. It's the authenticity of who you are that you need to project on the phone.'"

Wallace says each caller had a prayer partner. The partners prayed that God would help the callers convey caring and that God would give "listening ears" to the persons called. "The power of prayer was one of the reasons for our success," says Wallace.

Callers were given these guidelines:
- When someone answers the phone, immediately tell him or her your name and explain that you are from the church.
- Politely ask if it is a convenient time for a two- or three-minute visit.
- If the person called says it is not, say "Thanks," and end the call.
- If he or she says it's convenient, ask, "Are you active in a church?"
- If the respondent says yes, tell him or her you are happy about that, and say goodbye.
- If the respondent is not active in a church, ask if you can mail information about the new church.
- If the person says no, then thank him or her for the time.
- If the person wants more information, place his or her name and address on the prospect list.

Phone numbers given to each caller had been obtained from a city directory that lists telephone numbers by streets. R. L. Polk and Company publishes city directories. Most public libraries keep a current issue.

Wallace had defined homes within a four and one-half mile radius as the target area. The 160 volunteers made 17,000 phone calls. Of the 17,000 people who were called, 1,752 said they would like more information.

"We sent prospects three pieces of mail," says Wallace. "The first said, 'Thanks for talking with us on the phone,' and briefly introduced the church. The next was an attractive card that explained more about the church. Finally, we sent a letter and a magnet imprinted with our church's name and phone number. We encouraged people to put the magnet on their refrigerators or some other visible place."

The next contact was by phone. "We called all the prospects a second time and invited them to our first worship service. Then we sent each prospect a personalized, handwritten invitation. Those who responded favorably were called and asked if they would help with the first worship service. Some agreed to bring refreshments."

The first service was on December 3, 1989, and attendance was 235. Of that number, 30 were Cumberland Presbyterians from out of town who wanted to be part of the service. The other 205 were prospects.

Attendance the next Sunday was 150. By June 1990, the church was serving about 145 people. Average attendance was 80, and the church was continuing to grow.

Wallace says very few of the people they called seemed to be bothered by the calls; many told him the calls meant a great deal to them.

"One man said that, at the time we called, he was discouraged by problems he was experiencing. Although he and his wife had drifted away from church, they wanted to become part of one again, but they didn't know where to begin. We called when they needed us."

A single parent told Wallace that her eight-year-old daughter had asked her, "Mom, what's it like to go to church?" A few hours later the parent received the call from the church inviting her and her daughter.

Another woman said she and her family had lived in the area for five years and had never been invited to church. "We will be there," she said. And they were.

Wallace says there was one point in favor of having people from churches outside the area call long-distance. "We were networking in a broader area, and the total presbytery was involved."

However, he says having a local group make calls has more advantages in the long run. "After a caller makes twenty dial-ups and doesn't get a favorable response, it's easy for him or her to get a little discouraged. But if you have local people calling from a phone bank, callers can encourage one another when they get in a slump. When one caller has success, it encourages everyone else."

Wallace says the total cost for the prospecting campaign that launched his church was about $5,000—from start to finish.

Much of the cost was for the mailings, which Wallace says were an important part of the campaign. All the direct mail was printed on good quality paper with attractive artwork, and some pieces were done in two colors.

"Our phone calls and direct-mail pieces were the first contacts we had with people. These contacts made a statement about how we perceived our Lord and how we wanted to be perceived. We wanted people to know that caring and thoughtfulness go into everything we do."

Wallace strongly believes that churches must be concerned about the images they project in every contact they have with the public. "People are comparing you to the best, whether you are a church or a business," he says.

In addition to organizing the prospecting campaign, Wallace, with his wife's help, made about 850 phone calls—at least forty a night for twenty days.

"It was probably the most exhausting six weeks of my life," he says, "but we found it worthwhile. I highly recommend the telephone method to anyone who is prospecting for members."

Door-to-Door Distribution

First Presbyterian Church, Garden Grove, California, was actively involved in the life of its community, yet many people in the area were unaware of the church's existence, says Stephen Jenks, the interim pastor.

In January 1990, the four-hundred-member church launched an effort to inform the community about the significant programs it offered and to invite people who were not involved in church.

"We began by reviewing the needs of people in the community and what we as a church were doing to help meet those needs," Jenks explained.

Using a computer, desktop publishing software, a laser printer, and a high-speed copier, church members prepared a flyer on a sheet of legal-size paper. One side briefly described the church; the other side advertised an upcoming event that might interest people in the area.

Church leaders recruited about fifty volunteers from seven to seventy-plus to distribute the flyers. They gathered at the church for fellowship and training.

"We wanted everyone working on the project to understand our objectives," Jenks said. "We told them that our purpose was not to engage people in discussions about doctrine. Our purpose was to express the concern of the church. The most important things the volunteers could share about the church were their own experiences in it. They were not to explain Presbyterianism or argue with anyone."

Visitors knocked on every door. If someone answered, he or she was given a flyer. If there was no answer, the visitors attached the flyer to the doorknob with a rubber band.

Jenks says the church plans to distribute the flyers three or four times a year. The project has already had a beneficial impact in the life of the church. "Each time we do this, several families visit us. We find lots of new prospects. It doesn't cost much, and our members enjoy the work."

Mass Mailing

When Quail Springs United Methodist Church in Oklahoma City was being established in 1985, the church bought a mailing list for two zip codes in the target area. Two weeks before the first church service, leaders mailed a copy of the church newsletter to each of the 5,000 homes on the list.

The Rev. Tolbert Dill, the founding pastor, says several families came to the first service as a direct result of the newsletter. There were other benefits too. "When we went door-to-door, inviting people to the church, lots of people said they remembered receiving our newsletter. We weren't strangers to them. Their interest had already been stimulated."

Computers

Probably the best prospects a church has are its visitors, since many who visit are shopping for a church home. However, a church that has several visitors every week may find it difficult to keep up with them. That's why the

Prospecting for Members

Rev. David Severe, pastor of First United Methodist Church in Edmond, Oklahoma, started using a computer.

Dr. Severe had one of his members, who is a computer programmer, set up a program that keeps track of when visitors attend and when they are contacted. It also records information gathered by the pastor and laypeople when they contact visitors.

The program can match visitors with members who live in the same area, work in the same place, attend the same school, have children the same age, or have similar hobbies. It enables the evangelism team to make the best possible assignments as they decide how to follow up on prospects.

"We are still building our data base and refining our program, but it's already proving to be a tremendous help," says Severe.

Videotapes

A Disciples of Christ Church in Missouri uses videotapes as tools for prospecting and recruiting.

The church produces an orientation tape for prospective members. The tape—ten or twelve minutes long—shows scenes from worship services, Sunday school classes, youth activities, vacation Bible school, different age-level groups, and various ministries.

Volunteers take the tape to a prospect's home and say, "We would like for you to know more about us." They leave the tape and set a time to come back for it.

"Even if we never get the tape back, we have only three dollars invested in it, since we do our own duplication," the pastor explains. "The tapes really help prospects discover what we have to offer."

Audiotapes

Ridgecrest United Methodist Church in Oklahoma City gives visitors audiotapes to take home.

Each tape contains a greeting from the pastor, segments from worship services, choir specials, and one-minute statements from several men and women telling what they like most about the church.

Audiotapes are less expensive to produce than are videotapes, and they are easier to distribute by mail. The Rev. Don Horton, pastor of Ridgecrest, says he is pleased with the response the tapes have received. "They help people know that we would like to have them come back and be part of our church," he said.

CHAPTER 6

ADVERTISING EFFECTIVELY

In his autobiography, Benjamin Franklin says he never doubted that God exists, that God made and governs the world, that the most acceptable service of God is doing good to man, that our souls are immortal, or that all crime will be punished and virtue rewarded, either here or hereafter.

Franklin says he supported the only Presbyterian minister in Philadelphia, but spent his Sundays studying, rather than attending church. Once, after the preacher admonished him to attend, he went for five Sundays successively. Why didn't he continue? He candidly explains why.

The preacher's sermons "were chiefly either polemic arguments, or explications of the peculiar doctrines of our sect, and were all to me very dry, uninteresting, and unedifying, since not a single moral principle was inculcated or enforc'd, their aim seeming to be rather to make us Presbyterians than good citizens."[1]

Like Franklin, many people today who don't go to church probably assume they are not missing much. How can we get them to come? Not by laying guilt on them. We must convince them that they are missing something that can make a vital difference in their lives.

If we do have something vital to offer, then the next essential step is to let people know about it. How?

Church growth experts say that most people come to church because friends or relatives invited them. There's nothing new about this approach. It began when Andrew introduced Simon to Jesus, and it has carried the Christian faith from generation to generation for twenty centuries.

Advertising is no substitute for one-to-one evangelism, but it can reinforce the face-to-face efforts that members make, as the following case study indicates.

Case Study: Colorado Church

Hall Duncan, a church marketing specialist with headquarters in Harrison, Arkansas, recently helped a church in Colorado develop an advertising campaign.

The church, located in a town of 16,000 people, has 250 members, excellent lay leadership, and a dynamic pastor.

Advertising Effectively

To help members become more aware of the mission of their church, its strengths, and its uniqueness, Duncan spent a week at the church, attending Sunday school, worship services, and various group meetings. He visited with the pastor, key laypeople and a cross section of members.

At a congregational meeting, Duncan revealed what he had found and encouraged everyone present to respond to his observations.

Taking into consideration the responses made at the congregational meeting, Duncan designed several logos and slogans for the members to review. His intention was to help the members take a fresh look at their church and think about its mission, strengths, and uniqueness.

At another congregational meeting, he presented the logos and slogans. Members discussed them and selected the logo and slogan that they felt best represented what the church had to offer. They agreed to use the logo and slogan consistently on all signs, advertising, calling cards, and other printed material.

"Having a logo is like having a name," says Duncan. "Each church has its own personality; and a symbol is needed, not to take the place of the cross, but to help people recognize the church. It enhances the impact of advertising. When your literature goes out, people will begin to identify it with your church."

Duncan and a team working with him looked closely at the community—identifying needs, reviewing what the church was already doing to meet those needs, and considering what more the church could do. The team also considered trends in the community, such as changing values and lifestyles.

After studying the composition of the church and community, Duncan and the team identified a group of people in the community who might be interested in the congregation. The group became the church's target audience.

The team carefully reviewed every newspaper, radio, and television station to determine what medium would reach the target audience most effectively.

They then drew up an advertising campaign aimed at the target audience. Advertising copy was carefully designed to appeal to the interests and concerns of the specific age and interest groups in that audience.

The advertising campaign that Duncan drew up included a mix of radio and newspaper, along with a display ad in the *Yellow Pages.* Says Duncan, "All the ads were designed to say we are going to do the very best we can for Christ our Lord. We must put our best image forward at all times."

Within a few months after the first phase of the advertising had been completed, the campaign had already produced results. The number of first-time visitors doubled.

There were other benefits, too. The campaign stimulated the church to enter into new ventures. For example, it established a telephone hotline that is answered around the clock. Retired members take turns receiving the calls; then they channel them to care teams composed of laypeople who have expertise in various areas.

The church also developed seminars to help specific age groups—including single parents and senior adults—deal with the challenges they face.

Perhaps the most important benefit of the advertising campaign, according to Duncan, was the impact it had on members.

"We are hearing people say for the first time, 'Look, we know who we are, and we are proud of it.' Quality advertising builds healthful pride. It's like flying the flag."

The advertising budget for the Colorado church was $2,400 for 1990, about three percent of the annual budget. Leaders hope to increase the amount for advertising each year until it reaches seven percent.

"One option we are considering is a series of thirty-second radio spots just before the noon news," says Duncan. "We also may have a thought for the day—focusing on a Christian principle—during drive-time."

Duncan encourages churches to see advertising, promotion, and public relations as musts in today's world—as evangelistic investments.

"Lots of people out there will never be reached by the gospel of Jesus Christ unless we use the techniques that business and professional people use to sell products and services."

He emphasizes the importance of quality. "No businessman in his right mind would put up a shabby sign and expect it to bring in business; similarly, we should not expect shabby signs to produce good results for a church. A quality sign outside tells people to expect quality inside."

Duncan says many churches haven't been doing the job they should in glorifying Christ. "We've been settling for third best, making a crash program, getting something out. If the message of God's love is not precious enough for us to do a quality job, then I suggest that we not send out anything at all."

Advertising Guidelines

What follows are some guidelines based on Hall Duncan's model that can help your church get the best return from its advertising investment.

1. Identify the public that you hope to reach with your advertising. Don't expect to reach the general public; there is no such creature. Focus sharply on a segment of the community for whom you can provide a valuable service and from whom you have reason to expect a favorable response.

What group within your present membership are you now doing the best job serving? With whom have you experienced the highest degree of success? People who are of about the same age, income, and educational background, and who have similar attitudes, lifestyles, and theological views are probably the ones you should target. Go with your strengths.

2. Identify a need of the public you are targeting. Obviously, before you can address a need, you must identify it. That's why it's crucially important to understand what the people in your public think, feel, need, and want. Such understanding requires going beneath the surface—really getting to the hearts of the people. It means listening and looking.

The next step is to consider carefully what your church is doing or can do to help that public deal with hurts and hopes. There's nothing new about this strategy. Christians for centuries have followed Jesus' example of finding a need and filling it, finding a hurt and healing it.

3. Identify what your church has to offer people in your target audience that will help meet their needs. Ask members of your church who are similar to people in the target audience to tell you what the church has to offer. They may also provide testimonials that could be included in advertisements. You might even want to use one of them—or several of them—in your advertising.

4. Advertise when people in the public you are targeting are most likely to respond to what you have to offer. Timing has a significant impact upon the effectiveness of advertising. Many churches have the best results from advertising before Christmas, before Easter, and in the fall before school starts.

Several media planners have said they discourage churches from doing one-shot advertising. If you can't advertise with some degree of frequency, save your money.

Frequency is important for several reasons. In the first place, not everyone hears or sees an ad the first time it appears. So many ads bombard people each day that it is impossible to pay attention to all of them. Even if you have seen an ad many times, you may have absorbed little or none of the information. Therefore, one goal of frequency is to surpass the threshold, the first few exposures, so that the audience will absorb the message. Research has shown that there are threshold levels, although it isn't known precisely whether the threshold is two, three, or more exposures.

There are three main patterns that may be used in advertising. One—called the "straight-through method"—is advertising at a consistent level throughout the year: for example, having an ad every Saturday.

The second method—called "flighting"—concentrates advertising at certain times of the year, with no advertising at other times. For example, advertise before Christmas and Easter and in the early fall when school is starting, but do no advertising the rest of the year.

The third method—called "pulsing"—combines the first two. The advertiser does some advertising all the time and a lot of advertising some of the time. For example, have a small weekly ad in the newspaper to maintain presence; then advertise heavily before Christmas and Easter and in the early fall when school is starting.

Each method has advantages and disadvantages. The straight-through method enables you to maintain a year-round presence. The ever-present ad lets people know that your church is ever-present to serve—not just at Christmas and Easter. Buying a large block of advertising spread out through the year may also entitle you to significant discounts and more desirable positioning.

The flighting method helps stretch your media budget. You advertise when it is most likely to do you the most good. Dollars that you save by not advertising all the time can be invested in other media during the times you have chosen to advertise.

For example, if newspaper advertising is your basic medium, you might also use radio, TV, and direct mail during the times that will pay off best.

You risk overexposure when you use the flighting method. Your ads are likely to have diminishing return after people have seen them several times. Further, you risk underexposure the rest of the year, when you are not advertising.

Pulsing is probably the most effective of the three methods. Since churches are in business year-round, and since they do have seasons when they have more visitors who are shopping for churches, they need to maintain a year-round presence *and* increase advertising at the most propitious times.

5. Advertise in the medium most likely to reach the target audience. Since most churches have a limited number of dollars available, it pays to study options carefully.

Shop around. You may find that a thirty-second spot on the evening news at one TV station is $300, and a thirty-second spot on the evening news at another TV station is $400. Don't assume the $300 spot is the best buy. Check the ratings. You may find that the $400 spot is likely to reach twice as many people in the public you are targeting. On the other hand, the most expensive is not necessarily the most effective.

To determine where to place advertising, find out what papers people in your target audience read, what radio stations they listen to and when they listen, and what television programs they watch. Don't assume your favorite paper or station or program is the favorite of the public you are trying to reach.

Obviously, if you want to reach men between the ages of thirty-five and fifty, you won't choose to air during soap operas that come on during weekday afternoons. A better time would be during sports programs that air on Saturday afternoons.

A local advertising agency or media planner can help you decide where your advertising budget can best be invested.

When deciding where to advertise, remember that each medium has strengths and limitations. Let's compare advantages and disadvantages of the major media.

NEWSPAPERS

Advantages: Newspapers have a sense of immediacy, local emphasis, long life, flexibility, high-fidelity color inserts, and a mass reach.

Disadvantages: Ads are easily overlooked, especially by those who scan the paper.

Tips: Get the message into the headline. The headline should offer readers some benefit they want, and it should make the benefit sound as appealing and obtainable as possible. However, don't promise what you can't deliver. The copy should be as long as necessary to present the message, but no longer. Some studies show that long articles—assuming they hold the reader's interest—sell more effectively than short articles. The complexity of the message should determine the length of the ad. Keep it simple. Keep it interesting.

TELEVISION

Advantages: Your message is communicated by sight and sound, motion and emotion. Television is the next best thing to a one-to-one presentation. If what you have to sell can best be sold visually, television merits serious consideration.

The TV audience is vast. Nine out of ten homes have at least one color set. Moreover, we hear reports that sets are on, in the average household, six or seven hours a day. Programs tend to reach select audiences, thus helping you target your public.

Disadvantages: Television advertising is expensive—beyond the budgets of many churches. Production costs can be many times the cost of air time. Television commercials are easily overlooked or forgotten, simply because there are so many of them.

Before cable television became so popular, you had a good chance of reaching most TV viewers if you bought the same time slot on all three major network stations. This technique—called "roadblocking"—is not as achievable these days. Cable service subscribers can choose from at least thirty programs. Those with satellite receivers have even more choices.

The TV audience has also been fragmented by videocassette recorders (VCRs). Viewers can watch rented movies, or they can record a program and play it back at their convenience, fast-forwarding during commercials.

Tips: Since television is a visual medium, let visuals tell the story as much as possible. Show people, instead of buildings. Show people doing something interesting—having fun at church, working on a mission project, coming to grips with a social problem. Testimonials have possibilities. You might dramatize a typical problem to let viewers know the church can help them cope.

RADIO

Advantages: Generally, radio stations target selected audiences. Choose the station that targets the public you are trying to reach, and you may have the best advertising buy available. Audiences are often large—consisting of many who are in cars or at work. There are more than 400 million radios in the U.S., and the cost for radio time is relatively low. You can change the radio message quickly. Production cost is cheap compared with TV. Further, radio can be a good supplement to print advertising.

Disadvantages: The large number of radio stations—especially in metropolitan areas—creates a competitive problem. Audiences may be fragmented. Radio spots, like TV spots, are fleeting and may be missed unless the listener is keenly interested. Many listeners do not pay close attention. Usually, they are doing something else and playing the radio in the background.

Tips: Since radio provides no visual message, make full use of what it does provide: sound. Music can add impact.

A Baptist church in Oklahoma City produced a commercial with a catchy tune and simple lyrics. The church has aired it several times each week for a couple of years, and the pastor says it has contributed to several hundred people joining the church.

Since radio listeners have so many stations available to them, take extra care to select the station that will reach the public you are targeting. If you have produced a TV spot, chances are the audio portion will make an effective radio spot with little or no editing. Make sure, though, that the audio will carry the message.

Many churches across the nation are having excellent results from radio spots. An example is Central Lutheran, a 4,500-member church in Minneapolis, Minnesota.

The Rev. Stephen Cornils, the senior pastor, explains that Central, a downtown church, was having problems attracting people from the suburbs. In 1989, a member gave the church $50,000 for a radio advertising campaign. Two other members who are communications professionals volunteered to coordinate the campaign.

"We targeted young adults," says Cornils. "In May 1990—after the ad campaign had been underway for several weeks—the church received more than one hundred new members. Many of them had been drawn to the church for the first time by the ad campaign."

DIRECT MAIL

Advantages: No other advertising medium allows you more control in targeting a specific group of people. By purchasing mailing lists, you can mail to the specific market you want to reach, and your message can be targeted to their needs and interests.

Direct mail can be more personal than any other medium. Unlike radio and TV spots, it is not fleeting. People who receive it may keep a direct-mail piece for months. It is also easier to evaluate the results of direct-mail advertising, because you can trace it easily by coding.

Disadvantages: Direct mail can be the most expensive advertising medium in terms of the number of people you reach, because of the high costs of printing and postage. Keeping an accurate and complete mailing list can be a major expense and hassle. Delivery dates are also difficult to control.

Tips: Think through the objective, the offer, and the market before you begin writing. Show how your church can benefit the reader. If it takes more than one page to present your message effectively, don't worry. Studies show that a two-page letter often yields better results than a one-page letter. More people read short letters, but long letters sell more products. If you want readers, write short letters; if you want results, write as much as it takes to present your appeal clearly, concisely, and convincingly.

According to most direct-mail experts, third-class mail is usually as effective as first-class.

OUTDOOR ADVERTISING

Advantages: Outdoor advertising provides frequent exposure to a mass audience. The big print and attractive colors help capture attention.

Disadvantages: The message must be short and catchy. The cost may be prohibitive.

Tips: Since viewers are moving and (let us hope) not giving your sign their undivided attention, be brief. You have about ten seconds to get the message across. That's time for one strong picture and about seven words. Keep it simple; make it bold.

Advertising Isn't Enough

A major dog food manufacturer during the 1980s decided to put out a gourmet dog food. The company did extensive research. Pet owners said they would be willing to pay more for a top-quality product that would protect their animals' health. Veterinarians told company representatives what ingredients would provide the best nutrition. The company invested heavily in packaging and advertising, and the product was an instant success. But after a few weeks, sales plummeted. The marketing department couldn't understand what was wrong and started interviewing customers. Research revealed the problem: Dogs wouldn't eat the gourmet product, so their owners weren't buying it.

How does this relate to the church? A church can put together a program its leaders think people need. Advertising and promotion may get people to the church, but if the program isn't what people like, they won't return.

If your advertisng program isn't working, check it carefully; but don't stop there. Look at your church, too. The problem may not be the promotion. It could be that what you are offering isn't what people want.

CHAPTER 7

Enhancing Your Church's Image

Maxwell Maltz, a renowned plastic surgeon, has made us aware of the power perceptions have upon behavior.

"You act, and feel, not according to what things are really like, but according to the image your mind holds of what they are like," Dr. Maltz declared in his book *Psycho-Cybernetics*.

He explains, "You have certain mental images of yourself, your world, and the people around you, and you behave as though these images were the truth, the reality."[1]

"A human being always acts and feels and performs in accordance with what he imagines to be true about himself and his environment," concludes Maltz.

People who sell hamburgers and soap and cars and furniture and other merchandise spend millions every year trying to influence the perceptions people have of them.

Why? Because they have reached the same conclusion Maltz reached. They are convinced that how they are perceived determines how they will be received. Their sales records prove it.

Jesus, too, was concerned about image. "Who do people say I am?" he asked his disciples. Why did he care? He was no egomaniac, preoccupied with polls. Jesus cared about his image because he knew that people's perceptions of him would influence their response. What they thought about him influenced what they thought about the message he proclaimed.

Since people's perceptions of the church influence their responses, we have good reason to be concerned about the image our church projects.

How can we enhance our image? Here's how one Oklahoma City church did it.

Case Study: Wesley United Methodist Church, Oklahoma City

During the 1950s, when its membership was nearly 4,000, Wesley Methodist Church in Oklahoma City was regarded as one of the outstanding churches in Oklahoma. That wasn't the case in 1980. Membership, attendance, giving, and morale had dropped dramatically. So had the image of

Wesley. People said the church was dying. Since few people want to join a dying church, the future was bleak.

Part of the decline was attributed to changes in the neighborhood. Several hundred members of Wesley—many of whom were young couples with children—had relocated in new residential areas and were attending churches closer to their homes. Within a decade, worship attendance at Wesley had dropped from 602 to less than 300.

When the Rev. Robert Allen became the pastor of Wesley in 1982, only four children were in Sunday school. Two of them were his. However, by 1990, an average of sixty children were attending Sunday school. During those eight years, attendance at worship climbed from 300 to 475, and the annual budget grew from $200,000 to $475,000.

What made the difference? Leadership—pastoral and lay. Dr. Allen says the change was brought about by laypersons who were sold on the church and who accepted responsibility for selling it to others.

PROPERTY IMPROVED

During his second year at Wesley, Allen began encouraging the congregation to renovate the building. Built in 1928, the structure was basically sound, but practically every room needed repairs and paint. Restoration would cost at least a quarter of a million dollars. How could a struggling congregation come up with that kind of money?

Allen called a meeting of the executive committee and presented a detailed list of improvements that he felt were needed. The committee members looked at the list, made deletions and additions, then voted to move ahead.

One of the committee members, Jim Rice, a public relations and advertising professional, produced a slide presentation that made the congregation more aware of the need for restoring the building and helped them visualize how beneficial the improvements would be. The presentation was shown to every Sunday school class and small group. For five weeks, the public relations campaign continued.

On a date designated as "Miracle Sunday," members of Wesley were challenged to give the largest single gift they had ever given to the church. They were encouraged to contribute cash or anything that could be turned into cash. They came forward with stocks, bonds, cars, motorcycles, musical instruments—you name it. When all the items were turned into cash, the amount was $243,000.

The biggest miracle on "Miracle Sunday" was not the raising of $243,000, even though that's why national news services carried the story. The biggest miracle was the resurrection of hope and confidence. Wesley was alive, and members knew it.

The renovation project transformed Wesley's buildings, but it also transformed Wesley's people. They developed and displayed more pride. For example, a group of retired people took responsibility for the lawn. They planted flowers, set out trees, and built a little park.

NEW MINISTRIES LAUNCHED

The congregation also developed new ministries. Members started a handy-man service to help people in the congregation and community.

A decade ago, Sunday school, worship, and women's meetings were practically the only activities at Wesley. Today, 60 people are involved in the mobile meals program, 125 are involved in music ministry, 30 are "friendly visitors" who contact shut-ins. Scores of others are involved in various service programs.

The wide range of ministries provided by Wesley helps project the image of a caring church.

TELEVISION MINISTRY DEVELOPED

Allen earned the doctor of ministry degree at Drew University in Madison, New Jersey. His dissertation on how to develop a television ministry paid off when Wesley began a television ministry, airing the worship service weekly. Special gifts for the ministry enabled the church to invest $140,000 in cameras and editing equipment.

Television extended Wesley's ministry and enhanced the church's image.

STEPS TO A NEW IMAGE

Wesley's success is evidence that a church's image and its impact are related. Improve a church's image, and you improve its impact—and vice-versa.

Wesley's story also demonstrates that some of the basic steps taken to enhance the images of businesses can be used to enhance the images of churches. Here are some suggestions:

   1. Improve the appearance of the church's property. John F. Love, in his book *McDonald's: Behind the Arches,* says that Ray Kroc, one of the founders of the hamburger chain, created a family image for McDonald's by placing a high priority on cleanliness.

   According to Love, the 1958 manual that McDonald's operators followed specified that every day the windows had to be cleaned, the lot hosed down, and the garbage cans scrubbed. Every other day, all stainless steel in the store, including such typically ignored items as exhaust stacks, had to be polished. Every week, the ceiling had to be washed. Mopping floors and wiping counters became nearly a continuous process, and a cleaning cloth became an essential tool for every crew member.[2]

The appearance of property is important for a fast-food restaurant, and it is just as important for a church. When people pass by a well-kept church, they are likely to conclude that its members love it. On the other hand, if the lawn is full of weeds, if the building needs painting, and if the place looks abandoned, people will probably conclude that the church must not mean much to anybody.

Curb appeal makes a difference. Is your church dressed for success? Is it fit to be the Lord's house? What kind of image does it project? Does that image help sell your church to prospective members?

2. Provide a much needed community service. In his book, Love also says McDonald's discovered that "supporting a visible charity was not just a cheap form of advertising, it was better." Franchisers were advised to become involved with the favorite charities of their local newspapers—a surefire way of getting mentioned in the press coverage of any fund-raising activity.[3]

McDonald's sent press kits to operators suggesting how they might appeal to different markets and how they might get press coverage.

For example, during the 1950s, McDonald's managers toured Chicago's Loop in a vehicle called the "Santa Wagon," an ice cream vending truck converted into the rolling likeness of a McDonald's drive-in, complete with golden arches. The managers grilled hamburgers and made coffee; and at stops along the route they fed the street corner Santas of the Salvation Army. A photo of the Santa Wagon always made the Chicago papers.

McDonald's found that community involvement enhanced the restaurant's image: "It was an inexpensive, imaginative way of getting your name before the public," Love observes. He concludes that the company's early community service had a single motivation: selling hamburgers. He quotes McDonald's Fred Turner as saying. "We got into it for very selfish reasons."

Whatever the motivation, the community relations work has become one of the most powerful weapons in McDonald's impressive marketing arsenal, and it was individual franchisers who made it so.

Operators—not the company—developed and expanded McDonald's most visible charity: Ronald McDonald Houses. Located adjacent to children's hospitals, the houses provide free or low-cost room and board for families with children who need extended hospital care.[4]

In 1986, the year Love's book was published, there were one hundred Ronald McDonald Houses, serving more than 100,000 families.

While I do not advocate that churches become involved in community service projects just for free publicity, I do think churches need to be concerned about the images they project.

When people see that we are caring for those who are hurting, they are more likely to respond to our appeals. When we help people who are hurting, when we minister to them out of genuine concern and with professional expertise, we can make a difference in their lives. It doesn't hurt that we are also letting others know that we are there and that we are serving as God's agents of healing.

"Public relations is doing good and getting credit for it," Ralph Stoody, one of the pioneers of church public relations, said in the 1950s.

Jesus put it this way, "Let your light shine before others, so that they may see your good works and give glory to your Father in heaven" (Matthew 5:16).

How does a congregation project a new image? It takes more than glitter and gimmicks. The people have to break free from feelings of failure and futility and become aware that God can accomplish miracles through them. When people discover they can do all things through Christ who strengthens them, they push aside the barriers and boldly reach out with a joyful story to share.

When a congregation does that, the image of the church changes. People begin to say, "Something is happening in that church, and I want to be part of it!"

PUBLIC RELATIONS CHECKUP

Please read the following 12 statements carefully and circle the ones that you believe your church needs to give more attention.

1. Our members provide a warm, friendly atmosphere, and most people feel welcome and wanted.

2. We have a plan for discovering, visiting, and recruiting prospects for our church.

3. We try to enroll every church member in a class or learning group.

4. Persons each Sunday greet visitors and escort them to appropriate classes.

5. Our members are informed about programs and events that occur in our church and about the financial status of the church.

6. Our church has an attractive sign that identifies and informs the public about the times of services, the name of the pastor, and other important information.

7. Our church newsletter is informative, and it builds morale.

8. News of public interest is given to the local newspaper, radio, and television stations.

9. Our church property is well-maintained, and it presents an attractive image to the public.

10. Our building is used by or is available to community organizations.

11. Our church offers programs of interest and value to youth of the congregation and community.

12. Our church offers programs of interest and value to singles, older adults, and persons with handicapping conditions.

CHAPTER 8

MINISTERING THROUGH VIDEO AND AUDIO MEDIA

It's far more difficult to be a pastor in today's world than it was as recently as the 1950s, concludes Lyle Schaller.

In the first chapter of *It's A Different World,* the national authority on church growth and administration cites more than a score of changes that have enhanced the complexity of parish life and increased the difficulties facing the average congregational leader, either lay or clergy.[1]

In his second chapter, Schaller looks at the "sunny side of the street" and points to many ways today's world is far better.

His observations remind us that while today's church has more obstacles, it also has more opportunities. Even though selling the church may be more difficult than it was a few decades ago, never before have Christians had access to such tremendous technology for proclaiming the gospel.

Television

On May 27, 1990, I witnessed a miracle.

Inside the Oklahoma State Fairgrounds Arena, the Rev. Zan Holmes, professor of preaching at Perkins School of Theology at Southern Methodist University in Dallas, was delivering an inspiring sermon to about 5,000 people who had gathered for the opening worship service of the Oklahoma Annual Conference of The United Methodist Church.

Cox Cable was televising the service. The production truck was feeding the audio and video signal to the satellite "uplink" truck parked outside the arena.

I was sitting in the satellite truck, looking at two monitors. One monitor showed the video we were beaming up to a satellite. The other showed our program as it was being aired on a local television station. There was virtually no difference in the two pictures.

The operator of the satellite uplink didn't seem the least bit surprised that everything was working perfectly. "Once in a while we have a problem, but not often," he said casually. To me, it was a miracle. It was the first time I had been on the spot to watch a satellite transmission.

It was amazing to me that the audio and video were going 23,000 miles into the heavens to a Ku-Band satellite. A satellite service fifty miles from Oklahoma City was receiving the signal from the satellite, turning it around, and sending it to a C-Band satellite 23,000 miles away. The local television station was receiving its signal from the C-Band satellite. That means the picture I was seeing on the second monitor had traveled about 92,000 miles in less than a second.

The same signal was being picked up by another television station 100 miles away in Tulsa and by approximately 300 cable stations across the state that were part of the network we had organized. In addition, Cokesbury Satellite Television Network (CSTN) in Nashville was picking up the signal and sending it out to a nationwide audience.

I sat in the satellite truck, marveling at the miracle occurring before my eyes. I had no way of knowing who was watching or under what circumstances. I did know that scores of United Methodist congregations in Oklahoma were having worship services using our TV program, and I knew the program was being watched in several hospitals and nursing homes.

All kinds of people—in all kinds of settings and situations—were being united by means of TV. Never had I been more aware of the tremendous tool that television can be for proclaiming God's message of hope and joy and peace! Its potential is limitless.

What I witnessed reminded me of Bill Moyers' address in April 1990 at the Religious Communications Congress in Nashville, Tennessee.

"That little screen is the largest challenge God has given us in a long, long time," the prize-winning TV journalist said. "It can be the largest classroom and the largest cathedral."

Television can enable us to extend our ministries in many ways. Let's look at some possibilities.

TALK SHOWS

A talk-show format is relatively inexpensive to produce, but it can have a significant impact.

Since 1985, I have been the producer of a talk show called *Faith Factor.* Some of our guests are well-known; others are not. While they differ in many ways, they have one thing in common: faith in God has made a vital difference in their lives.

Dr. Norman Neaves, host of the program, helps our guests tell their faith stories. The program is taped at Church of the Servant in Oklahoma City, using volunteer camera operators, including one woman who is over the age of seventy. Tapes are aired on a network of cable stations.

PANELS

A panel program is another format that your church might consider. One church in Oklahoma City recently produced a program about coping with grief. The panel members who shared their insights included two pastors with extensive counseling experience, a medical doctor, and a psychiatrist.

DRAMAS

Dramas are more difficult and expensive than talk shows or panels, but they are a natural for television.

Monologues fit into this category. My colleagues and I produced one that has been well-received. Dr. Irving Smith, a retired pastor, did a series of twelve videotapes on characters of the Bible. Wearing appropriate costumes, he told, in first person, the stories of key biblical figures. His presentations have aired on cable systems in six states. Although we never advertised the tapes, we sold more than fifty sets to persons who inquired about them.

WORSHIP SERVICES

Broadcasting public worship services may not be the most creative way to use the intimate medium of television; however, don't underestimate the power of televised worship services. Each week, they enable thousands of people to participate in public worship, including those who are shut-in and those who feel shut-out.

The following case study shows how one church extended its ministry by televising its worship services.

First Presbyterian Church, Hollywood, California

First Presbyterian Church is less than two blocks from the famous Hollywood and Vine. However, in the past few decades, the neighborhood has changed dramatically. It is now one of the highest crime areas of greater Los Angeles. Even so, most of the 3,700 members of Hollywood Presbyterian drive from miles away, past scores of churches. What brings people to the church? Undoubtedly, one of the strongest appeals is its dynamic pastor, Lloyd John Ogilvie. Since his arrival in 1971, the church progressed steadily.

Television helped the church by attracting members and projecting an appealing presence. Approximately one out of five people who joined the church had the initial contact through television. The worship service is videotaped and aired locally and nationally on Trinity Broadcasting Network and other stations.

A thirty-minute weekly production, *Let God Love You,* helped the church establish ministries to people with special needs, including persons with AIDS, abused children, the homeless, the poor, and the emotionally disturbed.

Lane Adams, a former associate evangelist with Billy Graham, is executive producer of the program.

"What we are trying to do," Adams says, "is to record, as best we can within the time frame that we have, the dynamic of a life-changing message."

He says that the three cameras that are used to shoot the program are "eavesdroppers on the service." They are not on wheels or on a dolly, because moving them around could distract people in the congregation.

For TV viewers, it appears from time to time that the pastor is looking directly into the camera, but he isn't, says Adams. "We have one of our cameras about twenty-four inches above head level, and the two other cameras are a little lower; so when Ogilvie is looking at people in the sanctuary, given the distance of the cameras, it appears that he is looking into the camera."

The television ministry has nine employees and about twenty volunteers. They record services from September through June and use reruns from the middle of May through August. This enables them to build up a backlog of several programs to serve as a cushion in case an emergency occurs.

The television ministry at Hollywood Presbyterian Church operates as a separate nonprofit corporation with its own board of directors, and it is entirely supported by gifts from viewers. The budget for 1990 was $2,300,000. The pastor, Lloyd Ogilvie, doesn't take a salary from the television ministry and never has. In fact, he and his wife are among the program's top ten donors.

The church's literature and on-air appeals remind viewers that their first commitment financially should always be to their local church.

"As a pastor, Lloyd realizes how frequently the local church is robbed of its due because so much of what should be coming to it is going to 'parachurch' ministries, with no direct accountability to anyone," Adams explains. "If you have fulfilled your commitment to your church and find our program to be a blessing, then you are invited to support it. But never let your local church sacrifice for our needs."

Does this approach to fund raising work?

"We are not burning the woods down," Adams says. "But the response we receive shows that a lot of people appreciate the manifest integrity of our approach."

Adams says the program has a strong following among persons with higher than average academic achievement, position in society, and affluence. "That is sometimes the hardest group to meet," he adds. "Skid Row is not an address. It is a condition of the heart. Money, education, and position can anesthetize persons to the realities of their needs. Lloyd has a capacity to penetrate those needs."

The television ministry receives thousands of letters each year. Adams says church members constantly monitor responses to make sure evangelism and Christian nurture are taking place. "The mail bag is where we get our confirmation," he says.

What does it take to produce a television ministry that is worthwhile? "It takes more than tricks and techniques!" Adams declares. "Camera angles, special effects, gimmicks, voice inflection—that's not where it is. You had better have somebody who is powerful in the pulpit, in the exposition of Scripture, and in relating the message to people."

Adams is convinced that television can be a tremendous tool for ministry, but he has this word of caution: "I would not go near television unless I had seen evidence in my local congregation that lives were being radically transformed by the risen Christ through the ministry that is taking place in that sanctuary. TV time is just too expensive. It's not good stewardship to make it an ego trip or some sort of posturing of the local church to pretend to be more than it really is."

ELECTRONIC MEDIA INTERVIEWS

More and more pastors and laypersons are finding themselves in front of microphones and cameras, representing their churches on talk shows, discussion panels, news shows, or other radio and television programs. These appearances before vast audiences present tremendous opportunities for "selling the church." However, these appearances also present a terrific challenge, especially to those who are not accustomed to being "on the air."

Dr. Robert Grupe, a TV talk show host and the author of several textbooks about speech and communication, offers the following suggestions to help persons prepare for interviews.

- Get a feel for the interview setting. If time permits, visit the station a day or two before the interview and, if possible, walk through the TV interview stage area or radio station news area. If it is appropriate, visit with the individual who will be interviewing you. Engage in friendly conversation to set the stage for a relaxed and favorable later interview.
- Visualize the interview. Spend a few minutes in meditation—imagining the interview taking place. Think about possible questions and your responses. Allow yourself during meditation to feel the confidence and relaxation you want to feel during the actual interview. Create the scenario in your mind as though it were actually taking place. In so doing, you will program your mind to help you be relaxed and effective during the interview.

- Dress appropriately. What you wear should not attract attention to itself and away from you and your message. Gray, darker blues, yellows, and beiges are better colors to wear on television than white or black. Avoid wearing jewelry that jangles when you move or glares when you are under bright light. If you usually wear glasses, wear them for the interview.
- Remember, the microphone is your lifeline to the audience. Stay six inches to no more than a foot away from a stationary microphone for the best results. Resist the urge to shift your face away from the microphone to face the questioner. (You may be tempted to do so because the questioner is at an angle from the microphone.) For the best audio results, the lavaliere microphone (also called a lapel microphone) should be fastened about six inches below your chin on a tie, lapel, or blouse. Make sure the microphone is positioned so that it will not rub against your clothing and create objectionable noise.
- Watch your body language during the interview. Researchers say about ninety percent of the impression received during one-on-one communication is the result of body movements and tone of voice—not vocal content. Television puts you, the interviewee, into a personal, one-on-one relationship with the viewer. You are a guest in his or her home. Tension in your body will come across to the viewer. In many cases, tension will be interpreted as fear, uncertainty, or worse yet—defensiveness.
- Relax. Before the interview, sit or stand calmly for five or ten minutes. Breathe deeply; think pleasant thoughts.
- Be natural. Speak with the interviewer as though engaged in casual conversation. Weigh your words carefully, but do so in a relaxed manner. Do not droop your shoulders or bow your head during the interview; instead, keep your posture erect but comfortable. Pull your shoulders back and hold your head high so that your eye contact with the interviewer is at an even level. In doing so, you will create an air of relaxed confidence.

Video Recordings

In 1980, only two out of ten American households had videocassette recorders. By 1990, seven out of ten did. The number grew from 1.93 million to 66.3 million.

Obviously, this new technology has tremendous possibilities for ministry. Video productions can help "sell the church" by extending ministry within the congregation and community. What follows are some ways to use videos.

Spiritual nurture for shut-ins. Videotape your worship service and take the tapes to nursing-care centers, retirement homes, hospitals, and the homes of shut-ins. Don't limit yourself to worship services. Videotape solos, choir specials, and other musical presentations, or even Sunday school lessons. The possibilities are unlimited.

Video productions can be a two-way form of communication. For instance, you might interview a shut-in and ask her to tell how her faith in God is helping her cope with illness. Show the tape in her Sunday school class or in other small-group settings. Show it to other shut-ins. Put it in your archives.

Stewardship promotion. A fast-paced video report showing your church in action, enriching the lives of people in the church and community and beyond, can keep members informed, build pride in the church, and motivate members to support the church more generously and joyously with their time, talents, and money.

Preserving history. Tape three or four worship services and other special events every year and put them in your archives as historical records. To record living histories, interview people who have been involved in history-making events in the church.

EQUIPPING YOUR CHURCH FOR VIDEO MINISTRY

"As far as equipment is concerned, it's not what you have as much as how you use it that makes good video," says the Rev. Donald Wood, executive director of Good News Television Ministry (GNTM) in Macon, Georgia.

Under Wood's resourceful leadership, GNTM has developed extensive television ministries. In addition to innovative work in Georgia, GNTM has produced videos for mainline churches in locations across the U.S. and in more than ten countries.

Wood, a United Methodist clergyman, says churches should not shy away from using video because they don't have a fortune to invest. The kind of equipment you need depends upon what you want to do with it and how much of it you are going to do, Wood advises.

"There are home video camcorders in the $1,000 to $2,000 range that can turn out quality programs if you learn how to use them well."

Wood advises churches to check with local cable access about using editing equipment free or for a low charge. Another possibility is to contract for editing services.

"It's crazy to buy equipment to edit two or three videos a year that will be shown in homes or at the church. It's much cheaper to hire a production company to do the job for you, and you'll probably end up with a higher quality product."

If you are going to do a lot of video productions and are convinced that having your own equipment will be cost-effective, Wood advises to keep the skills of your crew in mind when making a purchase.

"If you have sophisticated folks who can use sophisticated equipment; if that's what you want to buy; and if you've got the money, then great. But don't buy a $50,000 paint box when you don't have someone who knows what it is."

Wood cautions that video equipment is "seductive" and can become a toy, rather than a tool for ministry. The latest models can entice people to upgrade equipment when doing so will not improve the quality of work.

Wood believes that the eight millimeter format has potential. A camcorder and editing system could be purchased for about $4,500 in 1990. The price might go down; electronic equipment costs have tended to decline in recent years.

To project the video to large groups, Wood thinks LCD projectors are the answer for churches. "You will be able to get them for $3,000. A church can put together a projection system for less than the cost of a new piano."

Video ministry has a spin-off benefit. "When churches use volunteers to do video productions, they discover people on the periphery of the church for whom video work offers an opportunity to use their understanding, interests, and technical expertise. The volunteers develop ownership in that program and in the church. They might never have taught Sunday school, sung in the choir, served on committees, or helped out in any other ministry."

The church should use the best communication forms available to pass along its values, according to Wood. "During Old Testament times," he says, "the part of the church that learned to tell stories passed those stories on from generation to generation, and their values became the values of society."

Video Production Process

Jesus reminded a crowd of followers one day that it pays to count the costs before making a commitment.

"If one of you is planning to build a tower, he sits down first and figures out what it will cost, to see if he has enough money to finish the job. If he doesn't, he will not be able to finish the tower after laying the foundation; and all who see what happened will make fun of him" (Luke 14:28-29, TEV).

There's a message in Jesus' words for anyone who is thinking about producing a videotape. Before deciding to produce a video, be aware of what it requires in terms of time, talent, and money.

It takes good equipment and people who know how to use it to produce a quality video, but that's not all it takes.

The first step—and perhaps the most important—in video production is writing the script, which serves as the blueprint for the production. Of course, the script cannot be written until you have answered such basic questions as:
- Who will be watching the video?
- Where will the video be viewed?
- What message do we wish to communicate to viewers?
- What response do we want viewers to make?
- What is the budget for this production?
- What is the deadline for the production?

Answering these questions requires research and reflection, as well as creativity. When the final draft of the script has been approved, the next step is to shoot video that will show what the script tells; then comes the editing process.

How much does it cost to produce a video? Just as the cost of building a house depends on the kind of house you build, the cost of a videotape depends on the kind you produce. If you hire a professional production company to do the job, the cost will probably be about $1,000 for each finished minute.

Radio

Television may be the dominant communications medium these days, but it is not the only medium; and it is not always the most effective medium for the church.

Radio has tremendous power to reach all kinds of people in all kinds of places and in a variety of ways.

"Radio allows you to play around more with the theater of the mind," says Tom Umbras, executive director of Ethnic Communications Outlet, a Chicago-based production company that has won more than fifty national awards for effective communications.

Umbras, a Catholic priest, shared some of his views about radio and how the church can use it effectively. He acknowledges that the choice of a communications medium depends on the message you want to communicate, the audience with whom you want to communicate, the budget you have available, and other factors. Each medium has its strengths and limitations.

"One problem I see with television," he said, "is that it packages everything for people. Our imaginations get lazy if TV is the only medium we rely upon. With radio, the imagination plays more freely. It has to create the images for itself. Radio respects a person's power to imagine values through song or drama. It frees people to see values in their own way, without imposing an image."

His specialty as a producer and director is creating life-situation dramas or mini-dramas that help people reflect on the human experience in light of the gospel.

Umbras suggests, "If you want to appeal to people, you have to know who they are and what they need and what they want. It's a matter of pinpointing your audience and identifying with them, then targeting their needs and values."

Umbras says it is important to be sensitive when working with ethnic minority groups. A member of a religious missionary order, he has invested most of his ministry with the Hispanic community in the U.S. and overseas.

"The church needs to be more sensitive to the needs and feelings of people in their culture," he says. "A lot of us are good at communicating what we want to communicate, but to make our communication work—especially with ethnic minorities—we have to listen."

"It's almost a religious experience when you can enter into other people's worlds and see what they see, feel what they feel, suffer their pain, and rejoice at their victories."

Umbras says too many media evangelists "push people into a mold and propose one-way communication." That's easier to do, he admits, than tuning in to the thoughts of the people to whom you are directing your message. However, if you want to get your message across, you must take seriously who is listening.

"It's very important to take people's life experiences as a point of departure and to lead them to see the faith dimension of their experiences," says Umbras. "You don't have to hit them over the head with the Bible to help them feel God's word for them."

Umbras' advice applies not only to radio, but to every medium of communication and to all the audiences with whom we communicate.

CHAPTER 9

UPGRADING CHURCH PUBLICATIONS

A United Methodist bishop told me that he spends about three hours every week reading newsletters from churches across his conference.

"I get about two hundred, and I glance at every one of them," he said.

How can a bishop afford to spend that much time reading what many people consider to be junk mail?

"Newsletters are the best source I have of finding out what's really happening in a church," explained the bishop.

"I find out quite a bit when I study a church's annual report, but the best way I've found to get a feel for what is happening is by looking at the newsletters week after week. A newsletter not only tells me what kind of programming a church has, it tells me what kind of spirit is there and what kind of leadership is being given."

Maybe it's unfair to judge a church by its newsletter, but plenty of people do, especially prospective members, inactive members, and disenchanted members.

People's perceptions of the church *will be* influenced by what they read in the church paper, and their perceptions will influence their response.

Church publications take time and money and hard work, but good ones pay for themselves. They help keep active members informed and motivated. In addition, church publications may be the only contact the church has with inactive and disenchanted members, some of whom may be trying to decide whether or not to come back. What they read may reassure them that the church cares about them.

Church publications—by presenting human interest features and member profiles—can build community by helping people become better acquainted with one another and more aware of their common concerns and commitments.

Administering the Church Publication

The church paper is the church's publication. It does not belong to the editor or the pastor, but to the congregation. However, since it is the official publication of the church, the officials of the church need to be involved in setting goals and policies and seeing that the goals and policies are taken seriously.

The first step in establishing or upgrading a church publication is to think through the purpose or mission of the publication.

The editor, pastor, and a few others may have a reasonably good concept of what the church paper is supposed to accomplish, but a few people with vague notions can't provide the foundation that's essential. The mission needs to be clearly defined, officially adopted, and well-publicized.

How do you get started? A communications committee (or whatever you choose to call it) should be officially appointed by the governing board of the church. It should be composed of people who are aware of and committed to the mission of the church. If they don't know the mission of the church, how can they know the mission of the church publication?

Church members who work in communications are prime prospects for the committee. It would be helpful to have representatives from various age-levels, but limit the membership to allow the committee to be creative.

The committee's first assignments are to brainstorm about the purpose of the church publication and prepare a mission statement. Committee members then present the mission statement to the policy-making board of the church for review and adoption.

Once a mission statement has been adopted, the committee has a guide for making important decisions, such as:
- Kinds of articles to be given priority
- Frequency of publication
- Extent of circulation
- Staffing
- Budget

The board needs to approve editorial policies that will clearly define the editor's authority and responsibilities. Recommendations for the policies should be prepared and submitted by the communications committee.

Most newsletters in churches with fewer than 500 members are probably prepared by the church secretary, with a little assistance from the pastor.

Putting out the paper is one of many jobs the secretary fits into an overloaded schedule. Deadline day rolls around, and the secretary discovers she doesn't have all the articles that should go in the issue. She makes phone calls, but no one is home. She waits for the mail to bring the promised articles. Meanwhile, a member drops by her office to visit. Emergencies arise. The pastor needs her to make arrangements for a counseling session, a meeting, or a funeral. There's a plumbing problem in the restroom, and she has to call someone to fix it. How can she concentrate on the newsletter?

Ideally, the church secretary should not have to be the newspaper editor. He or she has too many other responsibilities. The editing job is too important to be dumped on someone who is already overworked and who probably does not have the skill or the inclination to be an editor.

If the secretary would like to do the newsletter and has the skill to do so, but does not have the time, perhaps a volunteer could come in one day a week and take care of the office, providing time for the secretary to focus attention on the newsletter.

Many larger churches hire communications persons to edit the newsletter, send out news releases, coordinate the promotion of church events, develop audio and video resources, and help in other ways to promote internal and external communications.

Churches that cannot afford to hire someone might consider recruiting and training a volunteer—or several volunteers—to help with the job. Retired persons with expertise in communications may be available for moderate pay. A high school or college English teacher might find time to do proofreading. Even people who don't have specialized skills or training can be recruited to put on labels, sort by zip codes, and do other time-consuming tasks involved in preparing newsletters for mailing.

The point is, if the church is going to have a newsletter, it should arrange to have someone edit it who has the skill and time to produce a quality publication that will be informative and inspiring and that will project a positive image of the church.

Churches should provide editors with adequate tools to turn out attractive newsletters. If the budget does not permit the purchase or lease of dependable printing equipment, the church should consider using a fast copy service or print shop.

Competing for Readers

It's the end of a busy day. The prospective reader sits in an easy chair and sorts through what is available to read. Before her is *USA Today,* the current issue of her favorite magazine, a novel recommended by her best friend, and the church's newsletter.

What will she read first? At what point—if ever—will she pick up the church newsletter?

She may pick it up sooner than you think. Of all her reading material, the newsletter is more like a letter from home. It's about her church. It tells about activities in which she can participate. It contains names of people she knows—perhaps even her own name or the names of her children.

If a newsletter provides adequate coverage, is written well, and looks appealing, it has an excellent chance of being read. Readership surveys made by the Oklahoma Conference of The United Methodist Church Board of Communications indicate that quality church newsletters are read by as many as eight out of ten people who receive them. Here are suggestions for producing quality newsletters:

Determining Content

The mission statement of a typical church newsletter calls for the publication to provide information, promotion, inspiration, and community-building. Obviously, the editor should use these four objectives as a guide in determining what articles to publish. At least once a year, all issues of the newsletter should be reviewed to determine if the publication contains the appropriate mix of articles to accomplish its mission.

INFORMATION

Members have a right and a need to be informed about decisions the church administrators have made and about issues that are before the church. Whether the news is encouraging or discouraging, they have a right and a need to know about church membership trends, long-range plans, and finances. Generally speaking, the better informed members are about how the church uses its money for ministries, the more likely they will be to give generously and cheerfully.

The newsletter can and should provide such information in a timely and accurate manner. Of course, in order to inform others about what is going on, the one responsible for writing church news must know what is going on. Thus, the writer or editor must attend meetings, interview key leaders, and research church records.

Surveys indicate that readers are generally concerned most about what is closest to home. In keeping with that interest, a church newsletter should give prominence to the local church happenings, but it should also inform members about what other parts of the body of Christ are doing and what other pastors and laypersons are thinking and feeling.

Several hundred United Methodist congregations across the nation have local editions of the *United Methodist Reporter.* Local church news is on the front page; other pages contain news, features, and editorials from beyond the local church. After working closely with the *United Methodist Reporter* since 1977, I'm convinced that having a local edition of that paper is the best way for a United Methodist church to help its members see beyond their local concerns and realize they are part of a global church.

PROMOTION

Keeping members informed about activities of various groups within the church sounds simple, but sometimes it isn't.

On many deadline days, just as the editor finishes laying out the last page, someone runs into the office and frantically pleads: "We absolutely must have this article in this week's paper. It's about the biggest event we are going to have all year."

There's probably no way to eliminate all deadline violations, but here's a plan an editor might consider.

- At the end of this chapter are two forms. Make copies of each on 8½ by 11-inch paper, and use them as outlined below.
- Ask each group in your church to appoint a church newsletter reporter.
- Visit with each reporter individually. If that's not feasible, invite all reporters to a meeting. Review with them the publication's mission statement, the kinds of articles that are needed to accomplish the mission, deadlines, and other important guidelines.
- Ask each reporter to complete "Form A," which calls for basic information about a group's purpose, membership, and activities. Request that the form be submitted to you within ten days. When the forms arrive, file them in alphabetical order in a loose-leaf notebook binder under a section labeled "Church Groups."
- Give each reporter a supply of "Form B," and ask him or her to complete one for each event that his or her group would like the church's publication to promote. Request that the form be submitted as far in advance as possible to ensure the best possible coverage.
- Use a loose-leaf notebook to file the forms. File forms A alphabetically in a section labeled "Church Groups." Refer to it when you need background information about a group. File forms B in a section labeled "Events to Promote."
- Establish a column to be run in each issue that briefly describes events coming up within the next month. Refer to the forms in the "Events to Promote" section of your notebook for the details you need to write promotional articles.

INSPIRATION

The pastor's column in many chuch newsletters is inspiring, but other articles can also provide inspiration.

A timely "thought column" could be written by laypeople. Members can share experiences that have given them insights about life. In addition to being inspirational, such a column serves as a community builder, helping members become better acquainted with one another.

Another way to provide inspiration through the church newsletter is to report inspiring stories about projects and programs in which the church is engaged. For example, if a group of volunteers return from a mission trip to Bolivia, the editor could interview one or two of them and write an article—or a series of articles—that will inform and inspire readers.

COMMUNITY-BUILDING

The newsletter can help members of the church become better informed about one another, thereby building a sense of community.

Run profiles of members. A member with skills as a human interest writer could do a column in each issue—or when space is available—about an individual or family in the congregation. Prospects for such a feature might include key leaders in the church, Sunday school teachers, new members, long-time members, youth, older adults—the list could go on and on.

Many church newsletters include news about outstanding accomplishments of church members or their joys and concerns.

Writing for Print

A newsletter, as the name suggests, should contain *news*, and it should be written in the informal, personal style of a *letter*. Thus, when you are writing for the newsletter, write as you would write to a friend in the church (which is exactly what you are doing). Don't write to the "general public," which, as we have noted, doesn't really exist.

Although newsletter articles should be written in an informal style, they should not be thrown together hastily, without regard for effective communication.

Before writing an article, take time to answer these questions:
- What do I want to say?
- To whom do I want to say it?
- What response do I want readers to make?

Paula LaRocque, assistant managing editor and writing coach for the *Dallas Morning News*, has prepared a list of writing tips for reporters. The tips—presented below—are excellent for anyone writing for any print medium, including a church newsletter:

- Think. Writing and thinking cannot be separated. Fuzzy thought results in fuzzy writing.
- Get to the point immediately. Avoid irrelevant information.
- Avoid cliches, gobbledygook, "bureaucratese," "legalese" and other jargon, padded and bloated rhetoric. The more complex the message, the simpler the delivery should be.
- Attend carefully to mechanics: grammar, spelling, punctuation.
- Do not write to impress. Write to communicate.
- Generally, stick to subject-verb-object constructions. Avoid circumlocution, backing in, *non sequiturs.*
- Be suspicious of any lead sentence that begins with a preposition or verb. Such words necessarily begin clauses that are not the true lead. They soften and delay the lead, are generally less attractive than

subject-verb-object leads, and should be chosen only with specific intent.
- Prune excessive prepositional phrases. Several such phrases in one sentence can obscure the meaning.
- Strive for accuracy, clarity, and economy of phrasing.
- Search for the single right word to express your meaning rather than an almost right word modified, or a handful of almost right words. Cut out the use of vague qualifiers, such as *almost, rather, quite,* and *somewhat.* If you find the right word, you won't have to qualify it.
- Choose short sentences, but vary their lengths and structures so the work won't seem staccato, disjointed, and elementary.
- Work on transitions. Newspaper writing frequently omits them, but skillful transitions add immeasurably to polish, dimension, and meaning; and they speed the readers on their way.
- Beware of cute writing. It usually isn't.
- Maintain logic.
- Remember that the warning that we are writing for a grade-school reading level means in terms of simplicity, not sophistication; form, not content. We must, in all ways, be at *least* as intelligent as the reader.

Design

The content of a church newsletter determines whether it is worth reading. If it doesn't contain helpful information or insights or inspiration, if it is so unintelligible that readers must plow through it two or three times to unravel what it means, and if it's so dull they can barely get through it once, then a newsletter, like salt that has lost its flavor, is worthless. It is worthless even if it is laid out by an artist and printed in full-color on top-quality paper.

However, appearances do matter. If your newsletter is cluttered, full of typographical errors, and is difficult to read because of poor printing, then potential readers will conclude that it must not contain much of value.

Consciously or unconsciously, readers compare the church's newsletter with the professionally produced newspapers, magazines, and other print pieces that they receive. If the church's publication cannot compete for their time, they will be inclined to put it aside to read when they have nothing else to read; or they may pitch it in the wastebasket.

On the other hand, if the newsletter is appealing and looks as if it could be scanned easily, if potential readers can tell that someone invested a lot of thought and work in it, if it is apparent that the church thought it was worth doing right, then readers will likely conclude that it must be worth reading; and they will make time to read it.

The appearance of the newsletter is important because some members and non-members (especially) will form impressions of the church based on the publication. An attractive newsletter—like an attractive building—can help sell the church.

The following design guidelines can help make the church's publication more pleasing to the eye and easier to read.

- Determine what size paper will work best for your publication. Consider how much space you need and what kind of reproduction process you will use. After selecting the size paper, experiment with different ways to fold the sheet.
- Design a flag (nameplate) that projects an appealing image of your church. Perhaps there's an artist in the congregation who can assist. You might invite members of the church and people in the community to submit entries, and then present a prize for the flag that best captures the personality of your church. Many churches use color for the flag. The paper can be printed in large quantities for moderate costs.
- Place a masthead (informational material) inside the newsletter that lists the name, address, and phone number of the church, names of staff members, and times of services. Also include information about the newsletter—when it is published, guidelines for submitting articles, name and phone number of the editor.
- Keep the layout simple. Simplicity is the key to effective layout and design, just as it is the key to effective writing. The purpose of design is to help the reader get the message. It's not a place to impress people with artistic skills or with all the "neat things" a desktop publishing system can do.
- A dominant visual makes the page more interesting and gives a sense of order and unity. Every page should have one item—but not more than one—that stands out and grabs attention, and it should be the item that is important to most readers.
- Avoid static balance. Several elements that are the same size make a page boring.
- Place the most important elements in the upper left corner or the lower right of the page. Where articles are placed gives the readers a clue about their significance. Arrange elements so they will lead the reader's eye from upper left, across, and down the page.
- The headline should summarize the article in a few words—generally not more than seven. It should contain a subject and a strong verb. Subheads break up an article, help structure it, and make it easier to read.
- Select type carefully. Those of you who have typewriters or computers that allow you to change typefaces may be tempted to use four or five typefaces on a page just because you have them to use. If you do, your readers are likely to be distracted. Their attention may be diverted from the message to the type. Before using two or more typefaces in the

newsletter, examine how they look next to one another. Make sure they harmonize. There's only one reason for using types that don't have similar characteristics: to draw attention to one or two words by making them contrast. To ensure readability, select type that is large enough for most readers to see without straining. Avoid having lines of type that are too long or too short. Tests show that lines easiest to read are the width of a lowercase alphabet-and-a-half (39 lowercase letters) of the type being used.
- Use white space to highlight information. There's nothing wrong with a little white space, just as there's nothing wrong with a little silence. For maximum impact, have white space at the top, bottom, and outside edges of a page.
- As a rule, use white, ivory, or light gray paper and dark ink. Members of your congregation who have vision problems will be grateful.

PHOTOS

Newsletter editors may find the following guidelines for photos helpful:
- Use photos or clip art to communicate, not to decorate or fill empty space. If words can convey information or feelings more effectively or in less space, use words. If a photo is out of focus, poorly lighted, or otherwise lacking in reproduction quality, stick with words to tell the story.
- If you are going to run a photo, run it large enough to have meaning and impact.
- Edit a photo as you would edit an article. Cut out anyone or anything that does not add to the story. When cropping, avoid cutting off parts of hands, feet, ears, or heads. Do not include such small portions of objects that viewers will wonder what the rest looked like.
- Do not write on the backs of photos or put paper clips on them. Any indent in the glossy surface may show up in the reproduction.
- Every picture needs a caption. There's something wrong with a photo—or a joke—if you have to explain it, but photos often raise questions that need to be answered. The caption, rather than stating the obvious, identifies people and places in the photo and answers any questions that the picture might raise.
- Avoid using staples. They are difficult to remove without tearing the paper. Self-adhesive labels work well.

Taking photos for the newsletter can be a churchwide project. A wise editor will enlist volunteers. Here are some tips for those who take pictures for publication:

1. Get camera equipment that will do the job, and learn how to use it. A good choice for producing photos for the newsletter is a 35 millimeter compact autofocus camera. The camera is relatively inexpensive, easy to carry, simple to operate; and it produces satisfactory pictures for publication.

2. Use the appropriate film. Many photojournalists use black and white print films that perform well in low light and reproduce well for publications. There's something to be said, however, for color film if you are facing deadlines. Generally speaking, you can get color processed faster.

3. Focus your mind before you focus your camera. Before snapping the shutter, think about your objective and your audience. What's happening? Why is it significant? To whom is it significant? As the church photographer, try to be as inconspicuous as possible.

4. Compose carefully. Strive for alternatives to mug shots, handshaking rituals, and other overused and unnatural photos. Try to capture actions and expressions that convey what people are doing, feeling, and thinking. Look for the human element. Try to limit the number of people in each photo to four. When photographing groups, ask everyone to face three-quarters toward the camera and look at the lens. By doing so, they can get closer together and reduce the amount of lost space. To keep pictures from appearing static, make sure the focal point is not in the center of the viewfinder. Placing the subject slightly off-center creates visual interest. Imagine that your viewfinder is divided into three vertical sections of the same size and three horizontal sections of the same size. The points where the lines cross are called "hot spots" because they are good places to position the main attention of your photo.

5. Always take backup shots. Some professionals take twenty shots for every picture they expect to use in a publication. Shoot from different vantage points. Take vertical and horizontal shots so you will have options when you lay out your paper. Move around. Come in close.

6. Consider lighting. Photos will generally look more natural if you can avoid using a flash. Before resorting to flash, turn on all the lights in the room, open the curtains, get the subject closer to the window, go outside if that will help. Using a "fast" film and pushing it a stop or two can solve the problem. For example, if your film has an ISO rating of 400, set the ASA on your camera to 800 or 1600. Make sure you shoot the entire roll at the same ASA setting and tell your film processor what you have done, so necessary adjustments can be made in development.

POSTAGE

Keep in touch with the post office. Make sure you are following postal guidelines, and make sure the post office is handling your publication properly. If you receive reports that it is not being delivered promptly, document the problems and take them up with the postal authorities.

Upgrading Church Publications

Postage is one of the big cost factors for newsletters. The cost for mailing a publication that has been thrown together and is difficult to read is the same as the cost for mailing an attractive, informative publication. Costs for paper and printing are about the same, too, but there's a big difference in the payoff. The newsletter may be the primary contact some members and prospective members have with the church. Make sure it conveys the information and image that your church wants to convey. Make sure it says, "We care!"

FORM A:

ORGANIZATION DIRECTORY

Name of Group or Organization _____

Officers: Please give name, address, and phone number of at least two officers. _____, _____, _____

_____, _____, _____

_____, _____, _____

_____, _____, _____

_____, _____, _____

Meeting Dates _____

Meeting Location _____

Basic purpose for the organization _____

_____

_____

_____

_____

_____

_____

_____

Upgrading Church Publications

Form B:
Events to Promote

Name of event _____

Date _____

Location _____

Cost _____

Sponsoring group _____

Contact person for event (give name, address, and phone number of at least two people to contact for more information).

_____

_____

For whom is the event?

_____

_____

What is the basic purpose of the event? _____

_____

_____

Office use: List below when and how you plan to promote the event.

_____

_____

_____

Why Have a Church Newsletter?

1. What do you think your church newsletter should accomplish?

   _____
   _____
   _____
   _____
   _____

2. If your newsletter accomplishes what you think it should accomplish, what difference do you think it will make in your church and in the lives of people in the church?

   _____
   _____
   _____
   _____
   _____

3. What kinds of articles do you think will help accomplish the purpose of your newsletter?

   _____
   _____
   _____
   _____
   _____

CHAPTER 10

WORKING WITH THE MEDIA

Lee Iacocca of the Chrysler Corporation says that if he had to grade the business community on its cooperation with the press on a scale of one to ten, he would rate it about a two. "When reporters call for interviews, most companies tell them to climb a tree," he asserts.[1]

The relationship of the religious community to the press could also stand improvement. There's a chasm between the church and the public media, according to Tom McAnally, director of the United Methodist News Service.

"I hear complaints from church people all the time about the media," says McAnally. "Preachers say to me, 'The media don't understand us. All they are interested in is sensationalism.' Then when I'm in newspaper offices or television stations, I hear the other side. City editors and program directors tell me the only time they have contact with preachers is when the preachers want to complain about a story the media ran or didn't run, or when preachers ask for something for nothing."

The chasm that McAnally points to is not a recent development. Ralph Stoody, a pioneer of church public relations, was aware of it in the 1950s when he wrote *A Handbook of Church Public Relations.*

"Let's face it frankly," Stoody wrote, "while there are frequent exceptions, in general ministers and newspaper people do not understand each other too well." He said if the two professions had a better working relationship, both could produce better results for their constituencies.[2]

There's no reason for the church and the media to be adversaries. We can and should work together, but as Stoody pointed out, "We don't understand each other too well."

As church communicators, what can we do to improve media relations? I have posed that question to dozens of church communicators and media people. Based on their replies and my own experiences, I've got some suggestions.

DESIGNATE SOMEONE AS THE MEDIA CONTACT PERSON

Every church needs an official spokesperson to relate to the media. Why have one person assigned to the task? The media need to know with whom to speak when they are looking for official information about your church. If several people are reporting, the results can be confusing—especially if each is telling a different story. Furthermore, when several people speak for the church, each may assume that the other has spoken; thus, no one will speak.

The pastor or a staff member might be an excellent media contact person. However, a better choice is likely to be a layperson who is well-informed about the church and has the gifts and graces to present a positive image of the church to the media.

GET ACQUAINTED WITH MEDIA PEOPLE

The person who represents the church with the media can profit by getting acquainted with media people in the area.

Most reporters and editors are intelligent, creative, and caring. With few exceptions, they are genuinely interested in people and in what goes on around them. They must be to do their jobs well.

Generally speaking, media people—except for the stars—are underpaid and overworked. They hear lots of complaints and few compliments. Sometimes they must cover events that they would rather not cover. They are always fighting deadlines.

Since few media people have much time for socializing, the church representative may have difficulty becoming well-acquainted with them. However, efforts should be made.

Thoughtfulness helps build any relationship. To get along well with media people, remember that they are people. Be sensitive to the pressures under which they work.

More than a century ago, a reporter for a Boston newspaper wrote that when Phillip Brooks, who was then pastor of Trinity Church in Boston, walked through the newsroom, he lifted the spirits of everyone. Newsroom people of today could use a few church representatives like Brooks to lift their spirits.

PRODUCE A MEDIA KIT

A media kit can help the church contact person build a relationship with media people.

The kit should contain background information about the church, including the church's history, administrative structure, the church's mission statement, a glossary of terms distinctive to the denomination, membership data, church staff, hours of services, ongoing programs, and a photo and biographical sketch of the pastor. A list of suggested article ideas lifting up what is interesting and unique about the church might also be included.

Media kits don't have to be produced on expensive paper in full-color. Don't try to impress with frills. Let the contents convey the message.

The church's media contact should make an appointment to deliver the media kit. The contact should let the media know that he or she wants to establish mutually beneficial relationships. The contact should find out what kind of news the media want, when their deadlines are, and how they prefer to receive news leads. After the visit, the contact should write notes, expressing thanks for the media persons' time. The church's representative should maintain contacts with occasional phone calls or notes. He or she might even take media persons to lunch occasionally.

RESPECT DEADLINES

One of the best ways to show respect for media people is to respect their deadlines. For the newspaper to be delivered on time or for the newscast to begin on time, deadlines cannot be ignored. (Deadlines for undated feature material may not be as rigid, but these are usually set days or weeks earlier.)

If the church has promised a story to the local media at 3:00 p.m. on Friday, the story's publication or airing runs the risk of being postponed or canceled if it is turned in at 3:30 p.m. on Friday. Whoever handles the church's news releases must be prompt.

BE AVAILABLE

Church spokespersons should understand that media people operate on deadlines and sometimes need to contact them on short notice, or when they are in a meeting or having lunch. They should make every effort to be available. Spokespersons who do not return phone calls and who habitually make deliberate efforts to avoid the media are prime candidates for ambush interviews.

ACCEPT SPACE AND TIME LIMITATIONS

Virtually all news media are overwhelmed with more news, feature ideas, and information than they can possibly use in their limited time and space.

A church or any organization or individual cannot call the local editor and order a news story on page one. Certain rules and limitations are always in place that regulate what the reporter or editor can do.

DEVELOP A NOSE FOR NEWS

What is news to one editor or news director may not be news to another, and what's news to one editor or news director today may not be news to him or her tomorrow.

How do you determine what editors or news directors of local papers or stations want? Carefully examine what they use. Don't assume, however, that what they have been using is necessarily all they would consider using. If you have an idea for a different kind of story, present it.

Traditionally, journalists have used seven factors to determine news value:

1. Audience. Will our publics (readers, viewers, listeners) be interested?

2. Impact. How many people will be influenced by this event, and how significantly will they be influenced?

3. Proximity. Generally, the closer the event occurs to where readers live, the greater the news value. If you want to interest a paper or station in a national news event, your best bet is to present a local angle by showing how the event influences the community. Another way is to present a local reaction to a national event. However, don't manufacture a local angle when there isn't one.

4. Timeliness. The latest news is what interests people most. Today's headlines will be replaced by tomorrow's. For this reason, you need to plan ahead and submit article ideas while they are still news.

5. Prominence. People make news. The more prominent the people, the more prominent the story.

6. Unusualness. By its very nature, news is the unusual. If it is ordinary, it is not news. Something can be very important to the church—a great new program may have been launched—but it still may not be news to the community. Find a news angle. By being creative, you can usually find a way to lift up what is unusual. Within the congregation, there are probably scores of people who have unusual stories to tell. Submit tightly-written articles with human interest angles, and you'll be surprised how frequently they are used. If the church has unusual programs to address people's needs, program leaders will likely have insights to share that would interest the media. Present these ideas to local editors and news directors.

7. Conflict. If there's a fight—physical, verbal, ideological, any kind of struggle—it's likely to be news. This adds to the stress of being a church communicator. We would prefer not to have our church controversies aired. We would rather tell about the good things that are happening. Don't hold your breath for reporters to call for more details about the church's remarkable growth, the inspiring sermon that gave courage and hope to the congregation last Sunday, the marriages that the pastor's counseling has saved, or the bereaved people the pastor has comforted. However, don't be surprised if reporters call about a casual comment the pastor made about abortion, homosexuality, or some other controversial subject in the news. Conflicts are news.

Making the Most of Media Challenges

Concealed within virtually every crisis is an opportunity. Discovering that opportunity and making the most of it is a challenge.

This is especially true for what is often called a media crisis. Of course, churches have little risk of a media crisis if they stick to *sacred* matters—

Sunday school, worship, fellowship dinners, and maintenance meetings. The risk of a media crisis escalates sharply when a church is involved in the world. When it stands up for people who are being exploited; when it speaks out on controversial issues that influence humankind; when it embraces outcasts and heals them, a church is likely to experience persecution, just as Jesus did for similar offenses.

These days, churches and other institutions frequently face lawsuits because of alleged injuries or damages involving church staff, programs, or property. Lawsuits make news.

When the church is in the news because of some controversy, conflict, or allegation, its image is at risk. The risk is even greater in those rare instances when it seems that the reporter's primary mission in life is to look for, find, and expose scandals or stupidity in high or holy places. However, if the church spokesperson represents the church well, he or she can use these challenging times in the spotlight as opportunities to "sell the church" to members and the community.

During the decade that I have been media spokesperson for the Oklahoma Conference of The United Methodist Church, I have been involved in a dozen or so media challenges. Based on my experience and training, I have listed some suggestions that will help the church spokesperson respond effectively.

Prepare for the interview. The interviewer knows precisely what he or she hopes to gain. You as spokesperson should also have an objective. What two or three points should be communicated to the various publics of the church? Refine those points in writing—if possible—into several brief and convincing statements that will make memorable quotes. Use the statement as soon as possible in the interview and again when opportunities arise. Anecdotes and stories have power, assuming they are relevant and brief. Be well-informed. A crisis management team—consisting of five or six key administrators in the church—might help you gather all the essential information and plan a strategy for the interview. You should also prepare spiritually for the interview.

Approach the interview with a positive attitude. Think of the interview as an opportunity to "sell the church." Expect the interviewer to be fair; he or she probably will be. Try to develop good rapport. Use the interviewer's name occasionally and compliment him or her at least once, if you can do so honestly. Use personal pronouns. Humility and humor diffuse hostility, ease tensions, and build trust with the interviewer and the audience. Avoid arrogance.

Control yourself and you will control the interview. You cannot control the questions or the attitude of the interviewer, but you can control your responses. If the interviewer becomes hostile, look him or her in the eye, remain calm, and don't lose your temper. Let the interviewer know, however, that you cannot be intimidated. You are not on trial. Don't submit to being bullied, misrepresented, or abused in any way. Lean forward with energy toward the interviewer to assure him or her that you are not afraid. Don't shout. Speak clearly and at the same voice level you would speak to a friend a few feet away. Concentrate on every question and every statement that the interviewer makes. Think before you respond. Don't answer irrelevant or speculative questions. If the interviewer makes an inaccurate statement, ask him or her for the source of the information. After responding to questions, look for an opening to make one of the statements you want to make. You may even find a chance to ask a question of your own.

Be honest. To be honest, you don't have to tell everything you know. All you have to do is make sure everything you say—and every impression you intentionally give—is true. Never deceive or distort. If you don't know the answer to a question, say, " I don't know, but I can find out." If you are not free to disclose information, say that at this time you cannot answer and give a brief explanation, such as, "This issue is now in litigation," or "At this time, we do not have all the facts." Avoid saying "No comment." There are other ways of saying nothing that are less likely to arouse the suspicion of persons who are inclined to think the worst.

Process News Appropriately

What is the appropriate way to process news? That depends on the medium and the person with whom you are relating. Some prefer news releases; others, fact sheets. Some will take facts over the phone; others require that they be written. Ask each media person what he or she prefers.

To make sure you don't forget who likes what, prepare a page in your notebook on each medium. List phone numbers, contact persons, deadline information, and other specifics.

NEW RELEASES

A **news release** (see sample on page 92) is the format used most frequently to present stories to print and broadcast media.

Before writing a news release, get firmly in mind what you want to write, to whom you want to write, and why you want to write. List the items you want to include; then rank them in order of interest and importance.

Present what is most important or attention getting in the first sentence and follow with pertinent details in logical order.

Quotes—placed appropriately—add interest. Make sure they are accurate and attributed clearly.

Type the release double spaced on church letterhead or plain white paper, with margins one-and-a-half inches on all sides. If you use plain white paper, place an information block in the upper left corner. The block should give the name of the church on line one, the church address on line two, the name of the contact person on line three, and the phone number on line four.

If you want the release held for a few days, let the editor know by typing a release date on the right, a line or so below the information block. If the article is for immediate release, you don't need to specify. The editor will assume it is ready to release.

Headlines are optional. If you want to use one, type it in capital letters between the information block and the body of the release. It is customary for the length of the headline to be about the same length as the information block. For that reason, you may need more than one line for the title. If so, single space between the lines.

To allow space for the editor's comments, start typing the body of the release about one-third the way down the page. Indent paragraphs and double-space. If the release takes more than one page, indicate there is more by typing -*more*- at the bottom of the page. Start subsequent pages with a line (on either side of the page) that will identify the article and the page number.

To let the editor know where the story ends, type -*30*- or the word *end* on a line below the article.

When issuing a news release, send copies to all media. Generally speaking, don't give one paper or station preferred treatment. However, if you are giving a release to only one outlet, let the editor know by typing immediately below the release date the words *"Exclusive to"* followed by the name of the publication.

If the article you are submitting needs clarification, you might include a page or so of additional background information to help editors, news directors, reporters, and others who may be working with the news release.

News releases for the electronic media should be written for the ear instead of for the eye. The following are suggestions for preparing news releases for radio and television stations:

- Write conversationally. In conversation, for example, you don't begin sentences with long prepositional phrases; and you don't attach identifications at the end of sentences.
- Avoid abbreviations. They can confuse the broadcaster. Spell out the months and days of the year, titles, names of states, and names of organizations. Generally, the full name of the organization should be reported on first mention. Use hyphens between letters that are to be read separately.
- Keep numbers to a minimum. Radio listeners have trouble remembering them. The fewer figures you use, the more easily you will be understood.

- Identify names on first mention.
- Avoid lengthy quotes. Quotes will be understood better by the listener if they are paraphrased. However, in paraphrasing, be careful not to misinterpret the meaning of the speaker's remarks.

FACT SHEETS

Fact sheets often produce good results. List four or five events that are coming up at your church and describe each with a short paragraph.

The fact sheet is easier to prepare than a news release, and it often serves the purpose just as well. In fact, some papers and radio and television stations prefer receiving fact sheets because they can quickly determine whether any of the items interest them. If one does, a writer will be assigned to develop the story.

NEWS CONFERENCES

News conferences are a quick way to get information to the media, but do not schedule one unless the news you have to release is of major importance, will be of widespread interest, and must be released quickly.

If you hold a news conference, invite every medium that might have a legitimate news interest. Hold it at a location that will be as convenient as possible for the media, and make sure there are sufficient electrical outlets for TV and radio equipment. Pick a time for the conference that will allow most of the media to meet their deadlines.

The following additional suggestions will help ensure effective media relations:

Be brief. News media people need to know what they are wanting to know. Give them the facts quickly. Get to the point.

Be honest and accurate. There may be times when the media will ask questions that you cannot answer because you don't have complete information. Don't pretend you know more than you do. Explain that you will find the information and call them back; then do your research and respond promptly. That's how credibility is established, and credibility is crucial. Being honest and accurate builds goodwill that can make a vital difference, especially if your church experiences a crisis.

Don't bribe or threaten. Reporters and editors are human. Some will knuckle under to a free dinner or—heaven forbid—under-the-table cash. They are few. Those who follow the ethical standards of the media will be forever turned off to the church if someone tries to make deals.

Threats don't help either. Reminding the reporter or editor that your third cousin, twice removed, is a relative of the publisher or station manager is likely to create an embarrassing situation—as is threatening to cancel advertising in an effort to control or kill news coverage. If you are not pleased with an article, you'll accomplish little by scolding a reporter or reporting him or her to the editor.

Avoid getting carried away with public relations fervor. If your church has scheduled an elaborate Christmas musical, complete with special lighting, choreography, and a professional orchestra, and you bill it "the first of its kind," local reporters and editors are going to be "underwhelmed" when they recall that another church across town did the same thing last year.

If you want the media to take you and your church seriously, don't submit news releases when you don't have news. When you do have news to report, stick to the facts, unembellished with unbridled adjectives and unproved claims.

Buy advertising. When you prepare a news release, when a newspaper reporter interviews you, when a radio talk-show host asks you a few questions on a live broadcast, or when a television crew shoots footage of you and your church, you have little, if any, control over what will be used or how it will be used. Like it or not, that's the way it is.

However, if you don't like it, you have an alternative. You can buy space in the paper and time on the station; then you have control. You can do with that time or space just about anything you want. Rarely will the news media turn down paid space or time.

Express sincere appreciation. A thank-you note goes a long way. If you are grateful, say so. When you see a good article, even if it's written about another congregation, let the publisher or program director know that you appreciate good religious news reporting.

WORKSHEET

WHY TELL YOUR STORY TO THE COMMUNITY?

What can your church accomplish by keeping the public informed about its ministries, programs, and activities?

_____
_____
_____
_____
_____

List some ways your church can keep the public informed.

_____
_____
_____
_____
_____

Look at the above list and circle the items your church should give more attention to. How much do you think your church should spend for communicating with the public?

_____
_____

Working with the Media

WORKSHEET

HOW TO DEVELOP HEALTHY MEDIA RELATIONSHIPS

1. Put forth the effort to get acquainted with media people in your market who are assigned to church-related news.
   Respect them as people.
      They work for a living too.
   Respect their profession.
      The media have a powerful impact on opinion.
      Don't con them or court them.
      Think of them as partners, not adversaries.
   Respect their time.
      Don't drop in and expect them to drop everything.
   Respect their limitations.
      Policies restrict them.
2. Find out what they want.
   What is news to you may not be news to the media.
   To most journalists, news value is determined by
   - Consequence: Does it really matter to the media's public?
   - Interest: Will the media's public find it unusual, entertaining, inspiring, exciting?
   - Timeliness: By the time the "news" reaches the media's public, will it still be news?
   - Proximity: The closer the news, the more likely it will be to interest the media's public.
   - Prominence: If the news is about someone or something "special," it will be of greater news value. Keep in mind that what may be "special" to your church may not be special to the general public.

   One way to find out what media want is to study carefully what they use. Generally, what they use is what they want—but not always. The best way to find out what they want is to ask them.
3. Find out when they want news.
   Deadlines vary with publications.
4. Find out how they want news.
   Some prefer fact sheets; others prefer articles.
5. Give them what they want, when they want it, how they want it; then let them do what they want to do with it. If you don't want to leave the item in their control, buy an ad. Ads let you "do it your way."

Sample News Release

Name of the church
Address of the church
Name of person who is sending the release
Phone number

Release date

TITLE GOES HERE, UPPER CASE AND UNDERLINED

Dateline (the point of origin). Start the body of the news release about one-third the way down the page so the editor will have room to write instructions or comments.

Double-space the copy. Leave one inch to one-and-a-half inch margins on all sides.

Present the most important information first; then give the facts in descending order of importance. If there's not room for the entire article, it can be cut from the bottom with a minimum of editing.

If the release takes more than one page, write "-more-" at the bottom of the page and slug the following pages at the top left with a title followed by a page number. At the end of the release, type -30-, -end-, or #.

The most widely used public relations tool, a news release can help get your story told by newspapers, radio, television, and other media.

-30-

CHAPTER 11

SLOWING THE RUMOR MILL

I received a phone call the other day from a pastor who had heard a disturbing rumor.

"Do you know what Madalyn Murray O'Hair is up to now?" he asked.

Before I could reply, he began reading to me a letter that one of his members had passed along to him. It said O'Hair had been granted a hearing by the Federal Communications Committee (FCC) on Petition R.M. 2493 to stop all worship services from being broadcast by radio or television.

"There's a petition to sign and mail to the FCC," the pastor said. "Have you heard about this?" he asked.

I told him I had heard about it. In fact, every few months for the past decade, I have received calls or letters from pastors and laypeople who have encountered the letter. I told him not to worry, that it was a hoax.

The FCC says the rumor started in 1974, when two California men filed a petition urging the FCC to restrict use by religious organizations of FM frequencies reserved for educational use. Contrary to the rumor, the petition did not call for worship services to be removed from radio and television; moreover, Madalyn Murray O'Hair had nothing to do with the petition. Her name became attached to it, apparently, because she had won a Supreme Court decision prohibiting prayer in public schools.

In February 1989, the last time I talked with the FCC about the petition, I was told that the commission had received twenty-two million pieces of mail about the rumor.

"It's unbelievable," an FCC spokesperson said. "We have sent out press releases, notified papers all over the country—particularly religious publications. We've written churches. We've gone on TV. We've done everything we could to let people know there's nothing to this rumor, but the petitions keep rolling in. People have spent a fortune on postage; and there's no telling how much the FCC has spent processing the inquiries."

There's Nothing New about Rumors

Long before the dawn of the Information Age, rumors had a way of getting around with remarkable speed.

Jesus had to deal with rumors. His enemies spread rumors that he was a winebibber and a glutton, that he had spoken of tearing down the temple and rebuilding it in three days, that he had claimed to be king, and that he was guilty of blasphemy.

Rumors plagued Paul and other early Christians. In A.D. 64, when much of Rome was destroyed by fire, emperor Nero spread the rumor that Christians were responsible for the fire, and he had many of them killed.

About that same time, there were rumors that Christians murdered and ate infants. What was behind this rumor? References in the Lord's Supper to eating the "body" and drinking the "blood."

Still another rumor charged Christians with incest. How did that one get started? Christians who were husband and wife called each other "brother" and "sister."

Read biographies of church leaders—or biographies of any other leaders of any period, for that matter—and you will find that virtually all of them had to contend with rumors about their character, their performance, or their views.

Rumors can cause churches plenty of trouble. What's our best defense? Good character, good performance, and good communication—the three components of effective public relations—help, as the following case study illustrates.

CASE STUDY

It was Monday, and the Rev. Ben Jackson (not his real name) had been on the phone all morning, talking with angry church members about the youth meeting held the previous Friday evening at the church.

Callers said that they had heard that a local representative from a national organization often associated with abortion had presented a program about birth control and had offered to provide contraceptives to those who came to the office.

"Everyone in my Sunday school class is outraged about it," one caller said. "All of us think the youth director should be fired for inviting those baby killers to mix up our kids."

Jackson calmly assured his callers he would investigate and get back to them. He knew they were misinformed about what had happened at the youth meeting, but he knew he needed to get the complete story before making any replies.

He also knew he had a rumor on his hands. He was painfully aware that rumors in a congregation could start without due cause, undermine morale, destroy trust, shatter reputations, wreck careers, even cause some people to leave the church.

When Jackson talked with the youth director and others involved, he learned that a local representative from the national organization often associated with abortion *had* presented a program for the youth.

However, the allegations that the speaker had talked about abortion and had offered to provide contraceptives were not true. Instead, the speaker had talked about the physiological dangers of teenage sexual activity and had given the youth tips for protecting themselves from rape and incest. Parents of some of the youth had been present.

After gathering the facts, Jackson returned calls to everyone who had called him, told them what he had learned, and urged them to pass the facts to others.

He knew he also needed to reach persons who had not called him but who had heard the rumor or might yet hear it. How could he reach them? One option was to place an article in the church newsletter, denying the rumor. He discarded that idea because he feared that he would be spreading the rumor to people who had not heard it.

Jackson found another approach. He asked one of the parents who had attended the meeting and who was highly respected in the church to write an article telling about the meeting and how she felt about it. She did so. Her article described the meeting as a positive experience for the youth and parents. She said it was an example of how the church was addressing the needs of people and answering questions that were being asked.

After taking this action, Jackson didn't hear any more complaints. The rumor was killed.

Keep Rumors from Starting

When it comes to dealing with rumors, the adage that "an ounce of prevention is worth a pound of cure" certainly applies. We need to do everything we can to keep rumors from developing in the first place.

How can we? Here are some suggestions.

COMMUNICATE CLEARLY AND THOROUGHLY

Many—perhaps most—rumors develop because what is done or said is misunderstood. There is no malicious intent. Sometimes the problem is due to the failure to send clear messages. What is done or said comes across differently from what we think we are projecting.

In the church, there is a risk that some members will misinterpret the actions of the pastor and other leaders. Unless there is timely and thorough communication, some members may feel left out; and when they feel left out, they are likely to strike out. That's how rumors are born.

KEEP THE CONGREGATION INFORMED

Good internal communication helps a church reduce and dispel rumors.

Let's take another look at the rumor the Rev. Jackson and his church faced. How could it have been avoided? Good internal communication would have helped.

The youth director could have informed the pastor and other key leaders about the program that was coming up. Information about it could have been presented during board meetings. An informative article in the newsletter about the upcoming event might have prevented the controversy.

The church that accurately discloses all information that is of interest and importance to its members—including negative news that may disturb some people—will come out ahead.

BE CONCERNED ABOUT WHO WE ARE AND WHO WE APPEAR TO BE

How people perceive us determines how they receive us. If they trust us, they will be less likely to believe and spread rumors about us.

As church leaders, we must practice what we preach. Not only should we avoid doing or saying evil; but—as far as possible—we should avoid doing or saying what other people might perceive as evil. Paul's advice to the rumor-ridden church in his day is good advice for us too.

Of course, if we become too concerned about what people might think and what rumors they might start, we will never accomplish anything. We will become paralyzed by paranoia.

Coping with Rumors

Here's a four-step process—based on public relations procedures—that will help you deal effectively with rumors.

STEP 1. RESEARCH-LISTENING

When rumors are being spread about you or others, you'll feel the urge to do *something* immediately. Resist that temptation.

Before prescribing treatment, diagnose the condition. To slow or stop a rumor, you'll need to answer basic questions, such as:
1. What is the rumor? Are there several versions?
2. Is the rumor true?
3. Who started the rumor?
4. Why was it started?
5. How extensively has it spread?
6. What do our key publics think about it?

STEP 2. PLANNING-DECISION MAKING

After finding the facts and defining the problem, explore the options and decide what to do next.

If you find that a substantial portion of the rumor is true, admit the truth. By denying it, you compound the problem and add dishonesty to the other offenses. Next, outline the specific steps that will correct the problem and faithfully follow through on those steps.

Slowing the Rumor Mill

If your research indicates that the rumor is false, try to determine who started the rumor. You may discover that the rumor began when someone who didn't have all the facts simply got carried away by an overactive imagination and jumped to conclusions, never intending to harm anyone. If that is the case, encourage the individual to come forth and clear up the rumor.

If you find that the rumor was started by someone who was looking for a way to discredit the church, that information, if carefully documented, will be useful. In this age of litigation, proceed cautiously; you may need legal counsel.

STEP 3. COMMUNICATION-ACTION

If your research indicates that the rumor has not spread extensively and it does not seem to be disturbing your key publics, your best strategy may be to ignore it and hope and pray it will go away soon without doing too much damage.

Many rumors that circulate in a church can best be dealt with by doing nothing. Denying a ludicrous rumor that only a few people have heard and that not many are taking seriously may inform more people about the rumor, add credibility to it, and raise more doubts.

In many instances, a sense of humor is the best defense against rumors and gossip. Often, we take ourselves too seriously and become too concerned about what people think or say.

On the other hand, if a rumor is widespread and if it is being taken seriously by your key publics, you must respond. Your response should be carefully thought through, well-documented, and clearly presented.

STEP 4. EVALUATION

A good communications network can help you evaluate how well you have handled a rumor. Many pastors and laypersons in key leadership positions have found it helpful to have a few persons in the congregation who will provide feedback.

Stopping the rumor mill may be impossible, but good character, performance, and communication can slow it down.

There's another way to slow rumors: Before getting alarmed by a sensational story and before spreading it, do some research and listening. Resist the temptation to join in the witch hunt.

CHAPTER 12

MANAGING CONFLICT

In May 1990, two tribes in Papua, New Guinea, disagreed about how a pig should be served at a peace ceremony. Their squabble led to violence. Two thousand highland warriors fought from Sunday until Thursday, according to the Reuter news article reporting the event. When the fight finally ended, five people were dead and dozens were injured.[1]

It's difficult to believe that a disagreement over how to serve a pig could cause people preparing for a peace conference to kill one another. However, before we judge the tribes too harshly, let's consider what sometimes happens in our own churches.

Less than a week after the hostility in New Guinea, a conflict over church renovations led to violence in Melbourne Beach, Florida. One member of the building committee shot and critically wounded a woman, then went into the church and shot a deacon in the thigh, and finally killed himself.[2]

I've never seen bloodshed come from church fights, but I've seen more than one person leave the church in tears, vowing never to come back.

There are plenty of opportunities for conflicts to erupt in a church. In our pluralistic society, a church is a collection of individuals who have a wide variety of opinions on just about any subject. They have different—sometimes conflicting—interests and life-styles. Activities that one group considers important may be insignificant to another group. The generation gap can also create conflicts about what the church should do, when it should be done, and how it should be done.

A congregation in Tennessee wanted to buy a van to (among other things) provide youth with transportation to camps and outings. Younger women were frustrated—even angered—when an older woman remarked: "When my children were in youth activities, we mothers drove them where they needed to go. I don't know why mothers can't provide for their own children's transportation now!" Of course, she overlooked the fact that the mothers in the church, almost without exception, are employed full-time. Older women in the church also complained because the younger women refused to help cook meals at the church for various groups.

Have you had any conflicts in your church lately? I recently asked twenty-five pastors attending a public relations workshop if they had encountered conflicts in their churches lately.

They described seven conflicts:

1. A choir director was hired with the understanding that the congregation wanted traditional music. Because the director was so good, many new persons joined the choir. Some started pressuring for contemporary praise music. The congregation resisted; some left, and others threatened to leave. What should the pastor do to ease the problem?

2. A man in his late seventies with a great deal of verbal energy and anger disrupts and dominates every board meeting. He is a major financial supporter, and if he is offended, several key families will be upset. What should the pastor do?

3. A relatively small group in the congregation wants an evening service, and those members are vocal and insistent. They want a service each Sunday, but the pastor doesn't think the number of people who would attend the service would justify tying up every Sunday evening. Moreover, Sunday evening is the only time the pastor can do educational programming with the church. Since he is pastor of two churches, he feels he should be available for his other church on some Sunday evenings. He also wants to spend some Sunday evenings with his wife and children.

4. High school students who are drag racing on Main Street use the church parking lot as a place to turn around. They create a hazard for members coming to night meetings. Some of the youth are from prominent families in the community. How do officials of the church address the problem without creating enemies and a bad image for the church?

5. A child development center uses the fellowship hall and several classrooms during the week, which creates confusion and conflict over the use of facilities. The center provides a much-needed service to the community, and the income the church receives from it helps pay for utilities and repairs. How can the church officials promote better relations between the church and the day-care center?

6. The faithful pastor of seventeen years retired, and a new pastor was appointed. However, the former pastor and his wife have bought a home a few blocks from the church and remain active in the church. He has trouble resisting invitations to conduct weddings and funerals, and he continues to call on members in the hospital. How does the new pastor convince the former pastor and people in the church and community that there is new leadership?

7. A pregnant teenager wants to be married in the church. The pastor wants to be supportive of the girl and her parents, but does not want to disturb church leaders who insist that such a marriage cannot be held in the sanctuary or performed by the pastor. What should the pastor do?

As these examples illustrate, there are some points we need to remember about conflicts:

- Conflicts in a church are not always symptoms that something is wrong; they may be indicators that something is right. When everyone in a church agrees about everything that is happening, it's a sign that very little is happening, or that people really don't care what happens, or that they are afraid to disagree, or that they are convinced their opinions don't matter.
- Conflicts are not always destructive; they are sometimes constructive. They can motivate people to stand up and be counted, to do what needs to be done.
- Conflicts are not always about petty issues. Conflicts often arise concerning issues that will shape the direction of the church's ministry.
- Conflicts are not always motivated by a desire to gain or maintain power. Those who disagree are often motivated, not by selfish motives, but by a genuine desire to do what will help the most people. Reasonable people will have reasonable disagreements about how to solve complex and confusing issues that arise in a church.

Jesus—the "Prince of Peace"—avoided fights that could not be fruitful, but he did not flee from conflict when the time came for him to take a stand. Neither did Paul, Martin Luther, John Wesley, or Martin Luther King, Jr. Neither should we.

We should not "freak out" when fights break out. However, as church leaders—laity or clergy—we should do our best to minimize conflicts over trifles and to maximize the good that can come from conflicts that cannot be avoided. One way is to promote effective communication.

WHAT IS EFFECTIVE COMMUNICATION?

M. Scott Peck gives an insightful answer in his book, *A Different Drum.* He says if communication improves the quality of the relationship between two or more people, we must judge it to be effective. On the other hand, if it creates confusion, misunderstanding, distortion, suspicion, or antipathy, we must conclude it to be ineffective—even in those instances in which the communicator is evil, deliberately desires to sow seeds of mistrust and hostility, and may achieve that end.[3]

Peck says the overall purpose of communication is—or should be—reconciliation. It should serve to lower or remove barriers that separate human beings.

Effective communication calls for more than a good vocabulary and a mastery of grammar. It calls for an honest desire to help others understand what we have to communicate, what we think, and how we feel. We are not communicating effectively when we hide our real agenda, twist facts to fit our case, use misleading words, or drag red herrings by our audiences in hopes of leading them away from vulnerable areas or sensitive issues.

Managing Conflict

Effective communication is dialogue, not monologue; it requires listening as well as talking. To communicate authentically, we must sincerely want to get in touch with the needs and views of those with whom we are relating. We must be willing to let people express themselves—even when they disagree with us. We want to know what they think, where they hurt, and what they hope to accomplish.

Listening is not just being polite and letting someone else talk while we catch our breath and organize what we want to say. When we listen to other people—really listen with our minds and hearts as well as our ears—we are paying them high respect. We are saying, "What you think and how you feel matters. I care about you and respect you and want the best for you."

In a family, church, or anywhere else, when people really listen to one another, conflicts over trifles are less likely to occur, there are fewer misunderstandings, there is more harmony.

Effective communication is basic to being a good friend, to ministering to people, to building a good marriage, to developing and maintaining any kind of relationship. It's basic to managing conflict and building community.

How your church manages conflict will have a great deal to do with selling members and prospective members on the church. Most people aren't interested in being part of a church where people are caught up in power struggles and are fighting with one another.

If we practice the three essentials of public relations—good character, responsible performance, and mutually satisfactory two-way communication—in our churches, we will keep conflicts to a minimum and make the best of those that do occur.

Activity

Below is an activity to provoke thought and discussion. Even more important, it will encourage people to become more aware of the complex questions that pastors and other church leaders face.

The activity works best in a retreat or informal setting, but may be adapted to fit various settings.

- Write each of the seven conflicts mentioned earlier on its own index card. If you prefer, modify the situations or come up with your own.
- Divide your group into seven subgroups.
- Give a card to each group.
- Instruct each group to discuss the situation described on its card and to offer a solution, using basic public relations procedures (research-listening, planning-decision making, communication-action, evaluation).
- Invite each group to present its situation and solution. Allow members of the total group to offer their ideas.

- Have a couple of your most insightful members listen carefully to the discussion and identify key principles of conflict management that surface. Give them a few minutes to present the principles to the total group.

CHAPTER 13

INITIATING CHANGE

The Israelites faced grave risks when Moses urged them to follow him out of slavery in Egypt into freedom in the Promised Land.

We face risks as individuals and as churches anytime we consider making major changes. However, we must make changes if we are to stay alive and grow and achieve our highest potential.

How can we help our churches make the changes they need to make with the least amount of trauma and chaos? This success story offers some practical suggestions.

Case Study: Central Becomes Willowview

In 1981, Central United Methodist Church in Enid, Oklahoma, was in trouble. Attendance was half what it had been a decade earlier.

"The time had come for us to make a change," said Carl Christensen, a long-time leader of the congregation. "We were in the shadow of First United Methodist Church. It had 3,800 members, a magnificent building, and interesting programs for people of all ages. Prospective members could tell from the curb that First Church was alive, but when people passed by our church, they saw a deteriorating building with a dinky parking lot. If they came to our service, they found fewer than 150 people, most of whom were at least fifty."

Said Christensen, "We looked like a dying church. How could we compete? To attract new members, we needed better facilities and a better location."

Deciding to move wasn't easy, Christensen admits. "We were leaving a building that was paid for, and we were taking on a debt that would challenge us to the limit. We were also leaving behind a church home that was filled with memories."

Four years passed. On Sunday morning, February 24, 1985, nearly two hundred people gathered at Central for the official closing of the old church. After the call to worship, the pastor led the congregation in a prayer of gratitude for the blessings that had been experienced in the building. Then the congregation sang "Lead On, O King Eternal" and filed out. The custodian locked the door.

People got in their cars and formed a caravan to the new church, which was six miles away. The church had a new name: Willowview.

When people arrived, the custodian unlocked the door. The congregation entered and continued the worship service with a prayer of gratitude for the new church home.

Since moving to a new location, the congregation has grown substantially. In 1984, membership was 443. By January 1, 1990, it was 576. Average attendance at worship grew from 139 to 240. New Sunday school classes have been formed, and new activities have begun for all ages.

Suggestions for Making Changes

Christensen and other leaders at Willowview offer the following suggestions for congregations that may be thinking about relocating or making other major changes.

CATCH A VISION

"What do you want your church to be like in ten years?" the pastor asked Central's administrative board in 1976. The question started people thinking and dreaming, and a vision began taking shape. Many people could remember when the average attendance at Central on Sunday morning was 300, instead of 135. Members wanted the church to attract people of all ages. They wanted to reach out and grow as they ministered to others. Christensen says that without a vision, Central would not have taken on the risk of making a change.

RESEARCH CAREFULLY

The church leaders at Central carefully evaluated all options. Committees gathered demographic information from city planners, utility companies, and other reliable sources. Feasibility studies were made.

After the congregation decided to relocate, dozens of other decisions had to be made concerning the kind of building desired and the best way to finance construction. Each decision required days of research.

INVOLVE THE CONGREGATION IN DREAMING AND DECISION MAKING

From the very beginning, members were encouraged to express opinions, and their opinions were taken seriously, says Christensen.

Several surveys were taken. Members were asked, "What do you want your new church to be that it cannot be in this building?" and "What is there about our church as it now exists that you would like to see continued in our new church?" A committee reviewed the surveys and prepared summaries. "We tried to fit in as many of the suggestions as we could," says Christensen.

When it came time to give the new church a new name, members of the congregation were invited to make suggestions.

"Giving members an opportunity to express what they wanted in a church helped them have a sense of ownership," said one member. "I'm sure some people came with us who wouldn't have come if they had not seen that their opinions mattered and that the new church was going to be their church, just as the old one had been."

KEEP MEMBERS INFORMED

"We made sure the communication lines were always open," says Christensen. "We listened to suggestions and gave people a voice in what was going on. We also kept them informed about how we were coming along."

"The better people are informed," says Christensen, "the more likely they will be to understand the reasons for changes. The more they understand, the more supportive they will be."

BE PATIENT

"Many little crises came up along the way," said one member. "Every week brought a new problem. There were differences of opinion, but compromises were made. Our people always came through; they were never pushed or rushed. It takes time to work out all the complex problems. You have to be patient."

When the time comes for your church to make a change, the public relations procedure outlined below can help you minimize chaos and achieve the best results:

- Research—listening;
- Planning—decision making;
- Communication—Action;
- Evaluation.

CHAPTER 14

REFLECTIONS: IT WILL PAY OFF IN THE LONG RUN

When it comes to selling, the "old foot-in-the-door school of high pressure super-assertive techniques has gone the way of the dinosaur," says Marck McCormack in his book entitled *What They Don't Teach You at Harvard Business School.*

"Effective selling is directly tied to timing, patience, and persistence—and sensitivity to the situation and the person with whom you are dealing."

McCormack says it helps to believe in your product. "When I feel that what I am selling is really right for someone, that it simply makes sense for this particular customer, I never feel that I am imposing. I feel that I am doing him a favor."[1]

There's a message for us in his observations. Selling the church and proclaiming the gospel of Jesus Christ calls for timing, patience, persistence, and sensitivity to the situation and the person with whom we are dealing. We don't make disciples by bullying or bribing. We make disciples by being disciples.

It is vitally important that we believe in what we are "selling." If we believe that the gospel of Jesus Christ can help people experience life at its best and achieve their highest fulfillment, then we will not feel we are intruding when we invite them to invest themselves in Christ's service. We will know we are doing them a favor.

Let me share an experience I had while I was pastor at Lakeside United Methodist Church in Oklahoma City.

At the close of our worship service one Sunday morning in January 1979, I invited everyone who was interested in helping to recruit new members to come to the fellowship hall for a brief meeting.

Twenty or so came. I reminded them that church growth specialists say that most people who join a church came for the first time because they were invited by a friend. I asked them to think of one person—someone at work, a business associate, classmate, neighbor, friend, or relative—who was not active in a church, but might profit from being a part of Lakeside. I asked the members to invite those persons to come—better yet to bring them and then take them to lunch—within the next three months.

After the meeting was over, Lee White—who was very much sold on the church—told me he had already picked out 150 prospects and was going to

Reflections: It Will Pay Off in the Long Run

start inviting them immediately. But he said he was going to need some help with his plan.

Lee was 87 years old, and he didn't weigh much more than 87 pounds. A widower, he lived alone in an apartment less than a mile from the church. He had been a Certified Life Underwriter for more than fifty years, still had his insurance license, and still made sales occasionally. I knew he was a pro at prospecting, and I wondered what plan he had in mind for recruiting members.

"Nearly 150 people live in the apartment building where I live," Lee said. "Very few of them go to church. I think several would come here if they knew what they were missing by not coming."

Lee said he would invite every resident in the apartment building every week until Easter, if we would prepare flyers for distribution and if we would have a van at the building every Sunday morning to pick up people who wanted to come. "It'll pay off," he said.

Even though I had my doubts that his plan would pay off, I assured Lee that we would give him the help he had requested. On Monday morning, my secretary and I prepared the flyers, and I took them to Lee. That very day, he started going door to door, from the bottom floor to the top floor of the fourteen-story building. If anyone answered when he knocked, he handed him or her a flyer and invited the person to come to the church. If no one answered, he slid the leaflet under the door and continued on his way.

Lee called me Friday morning and said, "I've passed out all the flyers. You make sure the van is here at 10:30 Sunday morning."

The van arrived, but not a single person was there to ride in it.

"We'll try again next week," Lee said. "It may take awhile for this to catch on. But if we do it for six weeks, it'll pay off. You watch!"

The next Monday we prepared 150 more flyers and took them to Lee. During the week, he went to every door distributing them. On Sunday morning our van was there, but again no one responded.

Lee was still confident. "Several people have told me they are going to come," he said. "We are making progress."

The very next Sunday, our van did not come back empty. It brought Daisy Paris, a refined woman who appeared to be in her seventies. Lee sat by her in the service and introduced her to the congregation when we recognized visitors.

At the close of the service, I asked Daisy if it would be convenient for her if I dropped by her apartment for a visit. She said "yes," and we set a time.

When I visited Daisy, she told me she had worked twenty years as an assistant for Robert S. Kerr when he was governor of Oklahoma and when he was a U.S. Senator. She had never married and had no family in the area.

Although she had been active in church in her younger years, she had not attended church in quite awhile. In fact, she had not been going anywhere very much. She said she thought it was time that she got out again and that she would be coming back to church.

When our van arrived at the apartment building the next week, no one else was waiting for us, but Daisy was.

After she had been coming to Lakeside for about six weeks, Daisy told our driver that he did not need to come to the apartment building the next Sunday.

"Aren't you coming back to our church, Miss Paris?" he asked, obviously disappointed.

"Yes, I'll be there," Daisy replied. "But now that the weather is getting better, I can drive my own car. If others from here want to come, I'll bring them."

The next Sunday, Daisy drove her car to church. A week or so later, she joined the older adult Sunday school class. Soon, she was one of the class leaders. She and several other members of the class developed close friendships. They frequently shopped and ate lunch together.

About six months later, Daisy began to have severe headaches. When tests were run, doctors discovered she had a brain tumor. They operated and later administered chemotherapy.

During that long ordeal, members of our church—especially members of her Sunday school class—visited Daisy frequently and helped her in many ways.

While I was visiting with her one evening in the hospital, she told me she expected to die soon. She said she wanted me to tell the congregation how much it had meant to her to be a part of our church.

"I don't know how I could have gone through this," she said, "if I hadn't had the spiritual strength and the good friends that I found at Lakeside."

I assured her that she was a blessing to our church and that she was enriching our lives by sharing her life with us. A few days later, Daisy died.

We had not intruded on Daisy Paris when we invited her to Lakeside. We had done her a favor. Because she came, we were able to minister to her in a way that strengthened her for the ordeal she experienced during the final months of her life.

She was not the only one who benefited. Those of us who knew Daisy were spiritually strengthened by her, especially as we watched her fight courageously against cancer. Daisy had a tremendous impact upon us as individuals and as a church.

Her story illustrates something else, too: We cannot measure the value of our efforts by statistics.

Reflections: It Will Pay Off in the Long Run

Every week for two months, Lee White had gone from the bottom floor to the fourteenth floor of his apartment building distributing flyers. Our van had been there every Sunday morning, and only one person ever rode in it. But that one person was Daisy Paris.

It had appeared that we weren't going to accomplish anything with our recruitment efforts at the apartment building. Lee kept telling me, "It'll pay off in the long run." And he was right.

The truth is, anything we do to sell the church will be worth every dollar and every minute we put into it.

In his parable about the sower, Jesus made it clear that not everything we do will produce immediate results. Much will seem to fail, but what we do will be blessed. The harvest will be far beyond what we have ever dreamed. "It'll pay off in the long run."

ENDNOTES

INTRODUCTION

[1] Christian F. Reisner, *Church Publicity: The Modern Way to Compel Them to Come In* (New York—Cincinnati: The Methodist Book Concern, 1913), 5.

[2] Stewart Harral, *Public Relations for Churches* (New York—Nashville: Abingdon/Cokesbury Press, 1945), 16.

CHAPTER 1

[1] *Weekly World News,* vol. 8, issue 40 (July 14, 1987), 37.

[2] Theodore Levitt and Edward W. Carter, *The Marketing Imagination* (New York: The Free Press, Division of Macmillan, Inc., 1986), 142.

CHAPTER 2

[1] Viktor Frankl, *Man's Search for Meaning* (New York: Pocket Books, 1963), 121.

CHAPTER 4

[1] Harral, *Public Relations for Churches,* 24.

[2] Scott M. Cutlip and Allen H. Center, *Effective Public Relations* (Englewood Cliffs, NJ: Prentice-Hall, Inc., 1978), 16.

[3] Albert C. Outler, ed., *The Works of John Wesley,* volume 1, p. 105. Copyright © 1984 by Abingdon Press, Nashville, Tennessee. Used by permission.

[4] Richard P. Heitzenrater, *The Elusive Mr. Wesley* (Nashville: Abingdon Press, 1984), 156.

[5] Cutlip and Center, *Effective Public Relations,* 139.

[6] Robert T. Reilly, *Public Relations in Action* (Englewood Cliffs, NJ: Prentice-Hall, Inc., 1981), 12.

CHAPTER 5

[1] George Gallup, Jr. and Jim Castelli, *The People's Religion: American Faith in the 90's* (New York: Macmillan Publishing Co., 1989), 35-37.

[2] *Ibid.,* 29.

[3] *Ibid.,* 44.

[4] *Ibid.,* 88.

CHAPTER 6

[1] Benjamin Franklin, *The Autobiography of Benjamin Franklin* (New York: Collier-Macmillan, 1962), 81.

CHAPTER 7

[1] Maxwell Maltz, *Psycho-Cybernetics* (New York: Pocket Books, 1983), 34.
[2] John F. Love. *McDonald's: Behind the Arches* (New York: Bantam Books, 1986), 143.
[3] *Ibid.*, 212.
[4] *Ibid.*, 213-214.

CHAPTER 8

[1] Lyle E. Schaller, *It's a Different World* (Nashville: Abingdon Press, 1987), 18.

CHAPTER 10

[1] Lee Iacocca with Sonny Kleinfield, *Lee Iacocca's Talking Straight* (New York: Bantam Books, 1988), 156.
[2] Ralph Stoody, *A Handbook of Church Public Relations* (Nashville: Abingdon Press, 1959), 56.

CHAPTER 12

[1] *Daily Oklahoman,* 19 May 1990.
[2] *USA Today,* 22 May 1990.
[3] M. Scott Peck, *A Different Drum* (New York: Simon and Schuster, 1987), 257.

CHAPTER 14

[1] Marck H. McCormack, *What They Don't Teach You at Harvard Business School* (New York: Bantam Books, 1984), 92.

SUGGESTED READING

Beach, Mark. *Editing Your Newsletter.* Portland, Oregon: Coast to Coast Books, 1988.

Cutlip, Scott M., and Center, Allen H. *Effective Public Relations.* Englewood Cliffs, New Jersey: Prentice-Hall, Inc., 1978.

Gallup, George, Jr., and Castelli, Jim. *The People's Religion: American Faith in the 90's.* New York: Macmillan Publishing, 1990.

Newsom, Doug, and Scott, Alan. *This Is PR: The Realities of Public Relations.* Belmont, California: Wadsworth Publishing, 1985.

Reilly, Robert T. *Public Relations in Action.* Englewood Cliffs, New Jersey: Prentice-Hall, Inc., 1981.

Roman, Kenneth, and Maas, Jane. *How to Advertise.* New York: St. Martin's Press, 1976.

Schaller, Lyle E. *The Change Agent: The Strategy of Innovative Leadership.* Nashville, Tennessee: Abingdon Press, 1986.

Schaller, Lyle E. *It's a Different World: The Challenge for Today's Pastor.* Nashville, Tennessee: Abingdon Press, 1989.

Strunk, William, Jr. and White, E. B. *The Elements of Style.* New York: Macmillan, 1979.

_____. *Associated Press Stylebook and Libel Manual.* Reading, Massachusetts: Addison-Wesley Publishing, 1987.